STRESS MANAGEMENT AFTER GLOBALIZATION

Edited by

Dr. Rabi Narayana Misra
Roopesh Kumar Misra

DISCOVERY PUBLISHING HOUSE PVT. LTD.
NEW DELHI-110 002

Published by:
Tilak Wasan
DISCOVERY PUBLISHING HOUSE PVT. LTD.
4831/24, Prahlad Street, Ansari Road
Darya Ganj, New Delhi-110002 (India)
Phone: +91-11-23279245, 43764432
Fax: +91-11-23253475
E-mail: parul.wasan@gmail.com
info@discoverypublishinggroup.com
web: www.discoverypublishinggroup.com

***First Edition:* 2011**
ISBN: 978-81-8356-828-9

Stress Management After Globalization

Printed at:
Shree Balaji Art Press
Delhi

Preface

Stress is considered as a feeling of emotional or physical tension when faced with different situations. Stress is emotional physiological and psychological effects caused by internal or external mental pressure. Employers should provide a stress-free work environment, recognize where stress is becoming a problem for staff and steps should be taken to reduce stress. It reduces productivity, increases management pressures and makes the staff ill in many ways. It affects the performance of brain like reduces memory and work concentration.

So, some simple techniques are adopted to reduce stress. If these methods will be adopted by the managers of business organizations it will reduce the stress of the staff and it will help for increase of work performance. This book will help the managers of different organizations to reduce the mental tension. By using the simple techniques it will reduce the stress and relief the mental as well as physical burden.

Dr. R.N. Misra
MD Roopesh K. Misra

Acknowledgements

We are thankful to all contributors of this book. It is impossible in our part to edit this book without their active help and cooperation.

We convey our heartful thanks and express our warm gratitude to Mr. Tilak Wasan, Director of Discovery Publishing House Pvt. (Ltd.), Ansari Road, New Delhi for publishing this book without any hesitation. His son Mr. Parul Wasan and other members of the staff of Discovery Publishing House those who are actively involved in editing this book and publishing the book in time.

DR. R.N. MISRA
MD ROOPESH K. MISRA

Contents

Stress Management

*—Dr. Ch. Tirupathi Rao**

Stress can be defined as a state of physical and mental tension caused by certain external or internal factors in a person's life. The art of stress management is to keep yourself at a level of stimulation that is healthy and enjoyable. Life without stimulus would be incredibly dull and boring. Life with too much stimulus becomes unpleasant and tiring, and may ultimately damage your health or well-being. Too much stress can seriously interfere with your ability to perform effectively. By analyzing the likely causes of stress, you will be able to plan your responses to likely forms of stress. These might be actions to alleviate the situation or may be stress management techniques that you will use. Stress can have a great negative impact on your physiological as well as psychological wellness. At the same time, in modern life it is nearly impossible to avoid stress completely. Try what ever you may you are bound to feel stressed at one thing or another. It could be something that happened at the workplace, a child not performing well at school, the tiff that you had with your partner and various other such issues. Stress is part of your daily life.

* Reader in Commerce, Government Degree & P.G. College (Men), Srikakulam-532001, A.P. Accredited by NAAC with B++ Grade.

Identify the Sources of Stress in Your Life

Stress management starts with identifying the sources of stress in your life. This isn't as easy as it sounds. Your true sources of stress aren't always obvious, and it's all too easy to overlook your own stress-inducing thoughts, feelings, and behaviors. Sure, you may know that you're constantly worried about work deadlines. But maybe it's your procrastination, rather than the actual job demands, that leads to deadline stress.

To identify your true sources of stress, look closely at your habits, attitude, and excuses:

- Do you explain away stress as temporary ("I just have a million things going on right now") even though you can't remember the last time you took a breather?
- Do you define stress as an integral part of your work or home life ("Things are always crazy around here") or as a part of your personality ("I have a lot of nervous energy, that's all").
- Do you blame your stress on other people or outside events, or view it as entirely normal and unexceptional?

Until you accept responsibility for the role you play in creating or maintaining it, your stress level will remain outside your control.

People Most at Risk from Stress

In one U.S. study as many as 40 per cent of workers described their jobs as very stressful. While not a scientific gauge and not measuring serious stress health problems, this gives some indication as to how prevalent work-related stress is. As regards official health records, in the U.K., the nursing and teaching occupations are most affected by work-related stress, with two per cent of workers at any one time suffering from work-related stress, depression and anxiety. (The figure for teachers rises to four per cent when including physical conditions relating to stress.) Care workers, managers and professionals are the next highest affected occupations, with over one per cent suffering from serious work-related stress at any one time. UKHSE work-related stress statistics suggest that work-related stress affects men and women in equal numbers, and that people in the 45-retirement age suffer more than younger people. More socially-based U.S.A. research suggests that the following American social groups are more prone to stress (this therefore not limited to work-related stress): young adults, women, working mothers, less educated people, divorced or widowed people, the unemployed, isolated people, people without health insurance, city dwellers. Combined with the factors affecting stress susceptibility (detailed below), it's not difficult to see that virtually no-one is immune from stress. An American poll found that 89 per cent of respondents had experienced serious stress at some point in their lives. The threat from stress is perceived so strongly in Japan that the Japanese even have a word for sudden death due to overwork, *'karoushi'*.

Some Amount of Stress is Inevitable

Trying to remove stress from your life completely is impossible. A certain amount of stress actually helps in maximizing performance in specific situations. During times of stress, the human body reacts by releasing chemicals and other substances to reduce digestive secretions, increase heart beat and contract blood vessels. This state is called by various names like hyper-arousal, the acute stress response or the fight or flight response. These changes are intended to be temporary in nature to handle the stress situation that you are in. The body then needs to revert to its normal relaxed state. It is constant stress that causes the human body to be in a physiologically stressed state for a prolonged period of time &mdash something that can have a significant negative impact on your overall health.

Identify the Cause of Stress

The first thing that you need to understand to be able to manage stress is that stress is an individual experience. This basically means that the situations that cause stress are different for different people. While some people may not get worried about a child not being adept at sports, others may get extremely stressed out about the same. The circumstances that cause stress are based on individual perception and orientation. It is thus incumbent upon you and you alone to manage your stress by yourself.

Since the stress that you are feeling is so individualistic, the first step that you need to take towards managing it is to identify the *cause of the stress.* This needs a fair amount of introspection so that you can objectively and correctly identify the cause. Denial of a situation is something that needs to be avoided. Fooling yourself into believing that you are not worried about something, while in fact you are, will only make matter worse. Once you have identified the cause, it is also important to understand the various manifestations of the stress. Are you getting irritated with your wife just because your son is not skilled at football? Or do you seem to praise your son's friends excessively who are in the team?

Some Signs and Symptoms of Stress

- Tiredness/Exhaustion.
- Panic attacks and breathing difficulties.
- Insomnia.
- Irritability, impatience, angry outbursts.
- Pains almost everywhere, particularly digestive and abdominal.
- Increased reliance on alcohol, smoking, coffee etc.
- Muscle tension.
- Loss of or increased appetite.
- Anxiety.
- Grinding teeth/clenching jaws.
- Nervousness/trembling.
- Cold, sweaty hands.

The mind's reaction to stress is harder to predict. These mental reactions vary according to the situation and the person. They may include feelings of anger, fear, anxiety, annoyance or frustration. Prolonged stress is a serious condition can lead to life threatening illnesses particularly high blood pressure, stroke and heart attacks.

Unhealthy Ways of Coping with Stress

These coping strategies may temporarily reduce stress, but they cause more damage in the long run:

- Smoking.
- Drinking too much.
- Overeating or undereating.
- Zoning out for hours in front of the TV or computer.
- Withdrawing from friends, family, and activities.
- Using pills or drugs to relax.
- Sleeping too much.
- Procrastinating.
- Filling up every minute of the day to avoid facing problems.
- Taking out your stress on others (lashing out, angry outbursts, physical violence).

Stress Effects on Health and Performance

Stress is proven beyond doubt to make people ill, and evidence is increasing as to number of ailments and diseases caused by stress. Stress is now known to contribute to heart disease; it causes hypertension and high blood pressure, and impairs the immune system. Stress is also linked to strokes, IBS (irritable bowel syndrome), ulcers, diabetes, muscle and joint pain, miscarriage during pregnancy, allergies, alopecia and even premature tooth loss.

Various U.S. studies have demonstrated that removing stress improves specific aspects of health: stress management was shown to be capable of reducing the risk of heart attack by up to 75 per cent in people with heart disease; stress management techniques, along with methods for coping with anger, contributed to a reduction of high blood pressure, and; for chronic tension headache sufferers it was found that stress management techniques increased the effectiveness of prescribed drugs, and after six months actually equalled the effectiveness of anti-depressants. The clear implication for these ailments is that stress makes them worse.

Stress significantly reduces brain functions such as memory, concentration, and learning, all of which are central to effective performance at work. Certain tests have shown up to 50 per cent loss of performance in cognitive tests performed by stress sufferers. Some health effects caused by stress are reversible and the body and mind reverts to normal when the stress is relieved. Other health effects caused by stress are so serious that they are irreversible, and at worse are terminal.

Stress is said by some to be a good thing, for themselves or others, that it promotes excitement and positive feelings. If these are the effects then it's not stress as defined here. It's the excitement and stimulus derived (by one who wants these feelings and can handle them) from working hard in a controlled and manageable way towards an achievable and realistic aim, which for sure can be very exciting, but it would not stress. Stress is bad for people and organizations, it's a threat and a health risk, and it needs to be recognized and dealt with, not dismissed as something good, or welcomed as a badge of machismo - you might as well stick pins in your eyes.

Causes of Stress at Work

These are typical causes of stress at work:

- bullying or harassment, by anyone, not necessarily a person's manager
- feeling powerless and uninvolved in determining one's own responsibilities

- continuous unreasonable performance demands
- lack of effective communication and conflict resolution
- lack of job security
- long working hours
- excessive time away from home and family
- office politics and conflict among staff
- a feeling that one's reward reward is not commensurate with one's responsibility
- working hours, responsibilities and pressures disrupting life-balance (diet, exercise, sleep and rest, play, family-time, etc.).

Recognizing a Stressor

It is important to recognize whether you are under stress or out of it. Many times, even if we are under the influence of a stressful condition and our body reacts to it internally as well as externally, we fail to realize that we are reacting under stress. This also happens when the causes of stress are there long enough for us to get habituated to them. The body constantly tries to tell us through symptoms such as rapid palpitation, dizzy spells, tight muscles or various body aches that something is wrong. It is important to remain attentive to such symptoms and to learn to cope with the situations.

We cope better with stressful situation, when we encounter them voluntarily. In cases of a relocation, promotion or layoff, adventurous sports or having a baby, we tend to respond positively under stress.But, when we are compelled into such situations against our will or knowledge, more often than not, we wilt at the face of unknown and imagined threats. For instance, stress may mount when one is coerced into undertaking some work against one's will.

Learning Healthier Ways to Manage Stress

If your methods of coping with stress aren't contributing to your greater emotional and physical health, it's time to find healthier ones. There are many healthy ways to manage and cope with stress, but they all require change. You can either change the situation or change your reaction. When deciding which option to choose, it's helpful to think of the four As: avoid, alter, adapt, or accept.

Since everyone has a unique response to stress, there is no "one size fits all" solution to managing it. No single method works for everyone or in every situation, so experiment with different techniques and strategies. Focus on what makes you feel calm and in control.

STRESS MANAGEMENT STRATEGY AND TECHNIQUES

Avoid Unnecessary Stress

Not all stress can be avoided, and it's not healthy to avoid a situation that needs to be addressed. You may be surprised, however, by the number of stressors in your life that you can eliminate.

- **Learn how to say "no"** – Know your limits and stick to them. Whether in your personal or professional life, refuse to accept added responsibilities when you're close to reaching them.
- **Avoid people who stress you out** – If someone consistently causes stress in your life and you can't turn the relationship around,
- **Take control of your environment** – If the evening news makes you anxious, turn the TV off. If traffic's got you tense, take a longer but less-travelled route. If going to the market is an unpleasant chore, do your grocery shopping online.
- **Avoid hot-button topics** – If you get upset over religion or politics, cross them off your conversation list.

Alter the Situation

If you can't avoid a stressful situation, try to alter it. Figure out what you can do to change things so the problem doesn't present itself in the future.

- **Express your feelings instead of bottling them up :** If something or someone is bothering you, communicate your concerns in an open and respectful way.
- **Be willing to compromise :** When you ask someone to change their behavior, be willing to do same.
- **Be more assertive :** Don't take a backseat in your own life. Deal with problems head on, doing your best to anticipate and prevent them.

Adapt to the Stressor

If you can't change the stressor, change yourself.

- **Adjust your standards.** Perfectionism is a major source of avoidable stress. Stop setting yourself up for failure by demanding perfection. Set reasonable standards for yourself and others, and learn to be okay with "good enough."
- **Focus on the positive.** When stress is getting you down, take a moment to reflect on all the things you appreciate in your life, including your own positive qualities and gifts. This simple strategy can help you keep things in perspective.

Accept the Things you Can't Change

You can't prevent or change stressors such as the death of a loved one, a serious illness, or a national recession.

- **Don't try to control the uncontrollable.** Many things in life are beyond our control—particularly the behavior of other people. Rather than stressing out over them, focus on the things you can control such as the way you choose to react to problems.
- **Look for the upside.** As the saying goes, "What doesn't kill us makes us stronger." When facing major challenges, try to look at them as opportunities for personal growth.

- **Share your feelings.** Talk to a trusted friend or make an appointment with a therapist.
- **Learn to forgive.** Free yourself from negative energy by forgiving and moving on.

Make Time for Fun and Relaxation

Beyond a take-charge approach and a positive attitude, you can reduce stress in your life by nurturing yourself. If you regularly make time for fun and relaxation, you'll be in a better place to handle life's stressors when they inevitably come.

Healthy Ways to Relax and Recharge

- Go for a walk
- Spend time in nature
- Call a good friend
- Sweat out tension with a good workout
- Write in your journal
- Take a long bath
- Light scented candles
- Savor a warm cup of coffee or tea
- Play with a pet
- Work in your garden
- Get a massage
- Curl up with a good book
- Listen to music
- Watch a comedy.

Adopt a Healthy Lifestyle

You can increase your resistance to stress by strengthening your physical health.

- **Exercise regularly :** Physical activity plays a key role in reducing and preventing the effects of stress. Make time for at least 30 minutes of exercise, three times per week. Nothing beats aerobic exercise for releasing pent-up stress and tension.
- **Eat a healthy diet :** Well-nourished bodies are better prepared to cope with stress, so be mindful of what you eat. Start your day right with breakfast, and keep your energy up and your mind clear with balanced, nutritious meals throughout the day.
- **Reduce caffeine and sugar :** The temporary "highs" caffeine and sugar provide often end in with a crash in mood and energy. By reducing the amount of coffee, soft drinks, chocolate, and sugar snacks in your diet, you'll feel more relaxed and you'll sleep better.
- **Avoid alcohol, cigarettes, and drugs :** Self-medicating with alcohol or drugs may provide an easy escape from stress, but the relief is only temporary. Don't avoid or mask the issue at hand; deal with problems head on and with a clear mind.
- **Get enough sleep :** Adequate sleep fuels your mind, as well as your body. Feeling tired will increase your stress because it may cause you to think irrationally.

Quick Stress Reduction Techniques

If you are stressed, do one or all of these things, in whatever order that takes your fancy. These ideas can also be adapted for *team development exercises.*

The key to de-stressing in the moment is getting away from or removing yourself from the stressor. *Developing new habits,* which regularly *remove you and distract you from stressors* and stressful situations and pressures, is essentially how to manage stress on a more permanent basis.

In this modern world it is difficult if not impossible to change stressful situations. What we can do however is change and reduce our exposure to those stressful situations.

These stress reduction ideas and techniques are based on that simple principle. These tips won't change the situation causing the stress, but they will, more importantly, enable you to change your reaction and relationship to the stressful situations.

And in keeping with the tone of this stress tips section, and since colour is regarded by many as a factor in affecting mood, the calming shade of green is used for the headings.

Ways to Reduce Stress

- Identify causes of stress. Make honest assessments whether stress is related to your home and family, work or other relationship.
- Share your thoughts and feelings with your loved ones.
- Discuss the causes of stress, openly with those concerned.
- Try to avoid unpleasant situations.
- Realize that there are other people experiencing problems similar to yours.
- Simplify your life.
- Manage time and conserve energy. Make time for hobbies, recreational and social activities which will help divert attention away from problems.
- Follow a regular exercise programme. Practice a relaxation routine involving exercises, breathing patterns and meditations.
- Seek help from professional organizations or self-help groups which offers support and advise.
- Try to stay healthy.
- Avoid drugs and alcohol.

Stress Vs Time Management

*—Amrita Rani Misra**

Introduction

Stress Management is an important part of daily life for everyone. We all need stress in order to survive. Teams need it to perform well, and in the right doses, it can be very healthy, or even enjoyable. However, when stress becomes excessive it can be very damaging. It can harm:

- health
- happiness
- work performance
- team spirit and co-operation
- relationships
- personal development

Stress management involves, at the simplest level:

1. recognising the symptoms of stress
2. identifying the causes
3. taking action to address the causes and thereby reduce the symptoms
4. Where necessary, taking interim steps to relieve the symptoms until the underlying causes have been addressed.

* Lecturer in English, Mumbai.

There is Famous Notation

It is rightly said, "Time is life", "if you are wasting time—you are wasting life".

Level of Stress

The level of stress of every individual can be measured by following factors:

SPIRITUAL - identity, perception, values, self awareness.

MENTAL - thinking, discriminating, deciding, acting.

EMOTIONAL - feelings, emotions, intuition.

PHYSICAL - disease, illness, fatigue, food.

Symptoms of Poor Stress and Time Management

- *Irritability.* Fellow workers notice this first.
- *Fatigue.* How many adults even notice this?
- *Difficulty concentrating.* You often don't need to just to get through the day!
- *Forgetfulness.* You can't remember what you did all day, what you ate yesterday.
- *Loss of sleep.* This affects everything else!
- *Physical disorders,* for example, headaches, rashes, tics, cramps, etc.
- *At worst,* withdrawal and depression.

Principles of Good Stress and Time Management

- Learn your signs for being overstressed or having a time management problem. Ask your friends about you. Perhaps they can tell you what they see from you when you're overstressed.
- Most people feel that they are stressed and/or have a time management problem. Verify that you really have a problem. What do you see, hear or feel that leads you to conclude that you have a time or stress problem?

- Don't have the illusion that doing more will make you happier. Is it quantity of time that you want, or quality?
- Stress and time management problems have many causes and usually require more than one technique to fix. You don't need a lot of techniques, usually more than one, but not a lot.
- One of the major benefits of doing time planning is feeling that you're in control. Focus on results, not on busyness.
- It's the trying that counts - at least as much as doing the perfect technique.

Simple Techniques to Manage Stress

There are lots of things people can do to cut down on stress. The following techniques are geared to help you do what you know you have to do.

1. Talk to someone. You don't have to fix the problem, just report it.
2. Notice if any of the muscles in your body are tense. Just noticing that will often relax the muscle.
3. Ask your boss if you're doing OK. This simple question can make a lot of difference and verify wrong impressions.
4. Delegate.
5. If you take on a technique to manage stress, tell someone else. They can help you be accountable to them and yourself.
6. Cut down on caffeine and sweets. Take a walk instead. Tell someone that you're going to do that.
7. Use basic techniques of planning, problem solving and decision making.

   Concise guidelines are included in this guidebook. Tell someone that you're going to use these techniques.

8. Monitor the number of hours that you work in a week. Tell your boss, family and/or friends how many hours that you are working.
9. Write weekly status reports. Include what you've accomplished last week and plan to do next week. Include any current issues or recommendations that you must report to your boss. Give the written status report to your boss on a weekly basis.
10. "Wash the dishes". Do something you can feel good about.

Simple Techniques to Manage Time

The goal is set a reasonable amount of time to spend on these roles and then use that time wisely.

1. Start with the simple techniques of stress management above.
2. Managing time takes practice. Practice asking yourself this question throughout the day: "Is this what I want or need to be doing right now?" If yes, then keep doing it.
3. Find some way to realistically and practically analyze your time. Logging your time for a week in 15-minute intervals is not that hard and does not take up that much time. Do it for a week and review your results.
4. Do a "todo" list for your day. Do it at the end of the previous day. Mark items as "A" and "B" in priority. Set aside two hours right away each day to do the important "A" items and then do the "B" items in the afternoon. Let your answering machine take your calls during your "A" time.
5. At the end of your day, spend five minutes cleaning up your space. Use this time, too, to organize your space, including your desktop. That'll give you a clean start for the next day.
6. Learn the difference between "Where can I help?" and "Where am I really needed?" Experienced leaders learn

that the last question is much more important than the former.

7. Learn the difference between "Do I need to do this now?" and "Do I need to do this at all?" Experienced leaders learn how to quickly answer this question when faced with a new task.
8. Delegate. Delegation shows up as a frequent suggestion in this guide because it is one of the most important skills for a leader to have. Effective delegation will free up a great deal of time for you.
9. If you are CEO in a corporation, then ask your Board for help. They are responsible to supervise you, as a CEO. Although the Board should not be micro-managing you, that is, involved in the day-to-day activities of the corporation, they still might have some ideas to help you with your time management. Remember, too, that good time management comes from good planning, and the Board is responsible to oversee development of major plans. Thus, the Board may be able to help you by doing a better themselves in their responsibilities as planners for the organization.
10. Use a "Do Not Disturb" sign! During the early part of the day, when you're attending to your important items (your "A" list), hang this sign on the doorknob outside your door.
11. Sort your mail into categories including "read now", "handle now" and "read later". You'll quickly get a knack for sorting through your mail. You'll also notice that much of what you think you need to read later wasn't really all that important anyway.
12. Read your mail at the same time each day.

    That way, you'll likely get to your mail on a regular basis and won't become distracted into any certain piece of mail that ends up taking too much of your time.
13. Have a place for everything and put everything in its place.

That way, you'll know where to find it when you need it. Another important outcome is that your people will see that you are somewhat organized, rather than out of control.

14. Best suggestion for saving time-schedule 10 minutes to do nothing. That time can be used to just sit and clear your mind. You'll end up thinking more clearly, resulting in more time in your day. The best outcome of this practice is that it reminds you that you're not a slave to a clock - and that if you take 10 minutes out of your day, you and your organization won't fall apart.
15. Learn good meeting management skills.

    Meetings can become a terrible waste of time. Guidelines for good meeting management are included later in this section.

Effective Utilization of Time

Good time management is essential if you are to handle a heavy workload without excessive stress. By using time management skills effectively, you can reduce work stress by being more in control of your time, and by being more productive. This ensures that you have time to relax outside work.

The central shift of attitude within time management is *to concentrate on results, not on activity.*

To this end, it embraces a range of skills that help you to:

- Assess the value of your time, understand how effectively you are using it, and improve your time use habits;
- Focus on your priorities so that you focus on the most important jobs to do, delegate tasks where possible, and drop low value jobs;
- Manage and avoid distractions; and
- Create more time.

Time Management helps you to reduce long-term stress by giving you direction when you have too much work to do. It puts you in control of where you are going, and helps you to increase your productivity. By being efficient in your use of time, you should enjoy your current role more, and should find that you are able to find the time to relax outside work and enjoy life.

Techniques of Time Management

Some of the effective way of time management to reduce the stress

- **Plan each day** : Planning your day can help you accomplish more and feel more in control of your life. Write a to-do list, putting the most important tasks at the top. Keep a schedule of your daily activities to minimize conflicts and last-minute rushes.
- **Prioritize your tasks** : Time-consuming but relatively unimportant tasks can consume a lot of your day. Prioritizing tasks will ensure that you spend your time and energy on those that are truly important to you.
- **Say no to nonessential tasks** : Consider your goals and schedule before agreeing to take on additional work.
- **Delegate** : Take a look at your to-do list and consider what you can pass on to someone else.
- **Take the time you need to do a quality job** : Doing work right the first time may take more time upfront, but errors usually result in time spent making corrections, which takes more time overall.
- **Break large, time-consuming tasks into smaller tasks** : Work on them a few minutes at a time until you get them all done.
- **Practice the 10-minute rule** : Work on a dreaded task for 10 minutes each day. Once you get started, you may find you can finish it.
- **Evaluate how you're spending your time** : Keep a diary of everything you do for three days to determine how you're spending your time. Look for time that can be used more wisely. For example, could you take a bus

or train to work and use the commute to catch up on reading? If so, you could free up some time to exercise or spend with family or friends.

- **Limit distractions :** Block out time on your calendar for big projects. During that time, close your door and turn off your phone, pager and e-mail.
- **Get plenty of sleep, have a healthy diet and exercise regularly :** A healthy lifestyle can improve your focus and concentration, which will help improve your efficiency so that you can complete your work in less time.
- **Take a time management course :** If your employer offers continuing education, take a time management class. If your workplace doesn't have one, find out if a local community college, university or community education program does.
- **Take a break when needed.** Too much stress can derail your attempts at getting organized. When you need a break, take one. Take a walk. Do some quick stretches at your workstation. Take a day of vacation to rest and re-energize.

Time Management Matrix

	Urgent	Not Urgent
Important	I Crises Pressing Problems Deadline Driven Projects	II Prevention Planning Relationship Building Research
Not Important	III Interruptions Email Phone Calls Meetings	IV Trivia, Busy work Time wasters Pleasant activities

Conclusion

Some main ones why people find themselves too busy, along with time management and stress management ideas to help:

- **It's OK To Say No:** Many people end up overscheduling themselves because they feel uncomfortable saying "no" when people ask things of them. This may be because they don't want to admit to themselves that they can't "do it all," or perhaps because they don't want to disappoint others. Unfortunately, they ultimately disappoint themselves by not having enough time to do what's important to them. Does this apply to you? If so, learning to say no might be a good time management priority. Here's a resource on how to say no. Use it to create space in your schedule for what's important to you.
- **Be Clear On Your Priorities :** Others become over-scheduled because they add activities to their schedules for the wrong reasons, and end up spending their days doing things that don't reflect their values and priorities. Then they find themselves struggling to fit in what's important to them. Necessities like adequate sleep and other healthy habits fall by the wayside. Is this you? To find out, make a list of what's most important to you. List things like family, friends and career. Then look at how you spend your days. See how much time goes to these things. Is it a good match, or are you spending an inordinate amount of time doing things that aren't as important to you? It's never too late to make changes. (See this article for more on setting priorities in your schedule.)
- **Map It Out :** A common time management trap many people fall into is that they don't know where their time goes, or they overestimate the amount of time they have available and underestimate the amount of time each activity takes to complete, and become

overcommitted. How many times have you found yourself adding new activities to your schedule when you don't really know how you'll find the time to do them? If you remember several such instances, you may need to keep a careful schedule, writing down *everything* you do. Don't agree to new activities until you've found a way to pencil them in, overestimating the amount of time you think it will take to complete them.

- **Manage Money Wisely** : It's become increasingly common for people to work more than they'd like because finances demand it. Many people are working longer hours and even more than one job. Do you find that you're working hard to pay the bills, and when you're not working, you're still worrying about money? Do you know where your money goes? To get out from under debt and financial woes, you need a plan that involves spending less, saving, paying off debt, and possibly earning more (not by working *more* but by getting paid what you're worth). The Financial Stress section of this site can help you with all of that.
- **Stay Organized** : In addition to keeping an organized schedule, as mentioned above, it's important to maintain an organized home. Most people don't realize how much time and money are sucked up (not to mention stress created) by living in an environment where things are difficult to find and relaxation is a challenge. This section on staying organized can help you to stop the drain on your time that a messy home can create.
- **To Thine Own Self Be True** : Knowing yourself well can also help you to avoid getting overwhelmed. How? For one thing, by knowing your limitations, you avoid taking on too much. For example, if you know you're not the best manager of people, you can avoid putting yourself in a position where you'll be asked to do

management-type tasks, saving yourself stress and the extra time and energy it would take to learn to do this better. Also, if you constantly put yourself in a position of taking on more than you can handle, take an honest look inward to help you figure out what's behind this. That way, you can stop.

These resources should give you a good start on a less harried lifestyle. In the meantime, here are some stress relievers for busy people. They fit easily into a busy schedule to keep you more calm, cool, and collected.

REFERENCES

Cannon, W. (1939). *The Wisdom of the Body,* 2nd ed., NY: Norton Pubs.

Byrne, Rhonda. *The Secret,* Beyond Words Publication.

Mills, R.C. (1995). *Realizing Mental Health: Toward a New Psychology of Resiliency.* Sulberger & Graham Publishing, Ltd. ISBN 0945819781

Sedgeman, J.A. (2005). Health Realization/Innate Health: Can a quiet mind and a positive feeling state be accessible over the lifespan without stress-relief techniques? *Med. Sci. Monitor* 11(12) HY47-52.

Spence, J.D., Barnett, P.A., Linden, W., Ramsden, V., Taenzer, P. (1999). Lifestyle modifications to prevent and control hypertension. 7. Recommendations on stress management. The following techniques have been recently dubbed "Destressitizers" by *The Journal of the Canadian Medical Association.* A destressitizer is any process by which an individual can relieve stress. 160(Suppl 9):S46-50.12365525N.

Lehrer, Paul M.; David H. (FRW) Barlow, Robert L. Woolfolk, Wesley E. Sime (2007). *Principles and Practice of Stress Management, Third Edition,* pp. 46-47.

Stress Management and its Effects

—*Roopesh Kumar Misra*

Introduction

Stress is a normal physical response to events that make you feel threatened or upset your balance in some way. Stress is physical or emotional reaction/response to any kind of change-external or internal. Stress is a form of pain that comes to tell me there is something I need to change, Pain is a messenger that comes to tell me there is something I need to learn.

Body's Stress Response

When you perceive a threat, your nervous system responds by releasing a flood of stress hormones, including adrenaline and cortisol. These hormones rouse the body for emergency action.

Your heart pounds faster, muscles tighten, blood pressure rises, breath quickens, and your senses become sharper. These physical changes increase your strength and stamina, speed your reaction time, and enhance your focus-preparing you to either fight or flee from the danger at hand.

Stress response is the body's way of protecting you. When working properly, it helps you stay focused, energetic, and alert. In emergency situations, stress can save your life - giving you extra strength to defend yourself, for example, or spurring you to slam on the brakes to avoid an accident.

* Project Manager, Mumbai, India.

Stress response also helps you rise to meet challenges. Stress is what keeps you on your toes during a presentation at work, sharpens your concentration when you're attempting the game-winning free throw, or drives you to study for an exam when you'd rather be watching TV. But beyond a certain point, stress stops being helpful and starts causing major damage to your health, your mood, your productivity, your relationships, and your quality of life.

Causes of Stress

Situations and pressures that cause stress are known as *stressors.* We usually think of stressors as being negative, such as an exhausting work schedule or a rocky relationship. However, anything that puts high demands on you or forces you to adjust can be stressful. This includes positive events such as getting married, buying a house, going to college, or receiving a promotion.

What causes stress depends, at least in part, on your perception of it. Something that's stressful to you may not faze someone else; they may even enjoy it.

External Factors of Stress

Stress is caused by external factors.

- Major life changes
- Financial problems
- Work
- Relationship difficulties
- Being too busy
- Children and family

Internal Factors of Stress

Stress is caused by internal factors

- Inability to accept uncertainty
- Pessimism

- Negative self-talk
- Unrealistic expectations
- Perfectionism
- Lack of assertiveness

Common Symptoms on Stress

Stress mainly occurs as your body adapts to perceived physical threat, and is caused by release of adrenaline. Although you may perceive these as unpleasant and negative, they are signs that your body is ready for the explosive action that assists survival or high performance:

- Faster heart beat
- Increased sweating
- Cool skin
- Cold hands and feet
- Feelings of nausea, or 'Butterflies in stomach'
- Rapid Breathing
- Tense Muscles
- Dry Mouth
- A desire to urinate
- Diarrhoea

Performance Effects

While adrenaline helps you survive in a 'fight-or-flight' situation, it does have negative effects in situations where this is not the case :

- It interferes with clear judgement and makes it difficult to take the time to make good decisions.
- It can seriously reduce your enjoyment of your work
- Where you need good physical skills it gets in the way of fine motor control.
- It causes difficult situations to be seen as a threat, not a challenge.

- It damages the positive frame of mind you need for high quality work by:
  - ❑ promoting negative thinking,
  - ❑ damaging self-confidence,
  - ❑ narrowing attention,
  - ❑ disrupting focus and concentration and
  - ❑ making it difficult to cope with distractions
- It consumes mental energy in distraction, anxiety, frustration and temper. This is energy that should be devoted to the work in hand.

Physical Symptoms on Continued Stress

Where your body has been exposed to adrenaline over a long period. One of the ways adrenaline prepares you for action is by diverting resources to the muscles from the areas of the body which carry out body maintenance. This means that if you are exposed to adrenaline for a sustained period, then your health may start to deteriorate. This may show up in the following ways:

- change in appetite
- frequent colds
- illnesses such as:
  - ❑ asthma
  - ❑ back pain
  - ❑ digestive problems
  - ❑ headaches
  - ❑ skin eruptions
- sexual disorders
- aches and pains
- feelings of intense and long-term tiredness.

Symptoms shown Internally on Continued Stress

When you are under stress or have been tired for a long period of time you may find that you are less able to think clearly and rationally about problems. This can lead to the following internal emotional 'upsets':

- Worry or anxiety
- Confusion, and an inability to concentrate or make decisions
- Feeling ill
- Feeling out of control or overwhelmed by events
- Mood changes:
  - ❑ Depression
  - ❑ Frustration
  - ❑ Hostility
  - ❑ Helplessness
  - ❑ Impatience and irritability
  - ❑ Restlessness
- Being more lethargic
- Difficulty sleeping
- Drinking more alcohol and smoking more
- Changing eating habits
- Reduced sex drive
- Relying more on medication.

Behavioural Symptoms on Continued Stress

When you or other people are under pressure, this can show as:

- Talking too fast or too loud
- Yawning
- Fiddling and twitching, nail biting, grinding teeth, drumming fingers, pacing, etc.
- Bad moods:
  - ❑ Being irritable
  - ❑ Defensiveness

- ❑ Being critical
- ❑ Aggression
- ❑ Irrationality
- ❑ Overreaction and reacting emotionally

- Reduced personal effectiveness:
  - ❑ Being unreasonably negative
  - ❑ Making less realistic judgements
  - ❑ Being unable to concentrate and having difficulty making decisions
  - ❑ Being more forgetful
  - ❑ Making more mistakes
  - ❑ Being more accident prone
- Changing work habits
- Increased absenteeism
- Neglect of personal appearance.

Impact on Tolerance Level of Stress

- **Your support network** : A strong network of supportive friends and family members is an enormous buffer against life's stressors. On the flip side, the more lonely and isolated you are, the greater your vulnerability to stress.
- **Your sense of control** : If you have confidence in yourself and your ability to influence events and persevere through challenges, it's easier to take stress in stride. People who are vulnerable to stress tend to feel like things are out of their control.
- **Your attitude and outlook** : Stress-hardy people have an optimistic attitude. They tend to embrace challenges, have a strong sense of humor, accept that change is a part of life, and believe in a higher power or purpose.
- **Your ability to deal with your emotions** : You're extremely vulnerable to stress if you don't know how to calm and soothe yourself when you're feeling sad,

angry, or afraid. The ability to bring your emotions into balance helps you bounce back from adversity.

- **Your knowledge and preparation :** The more you know about a stressful situation, including how long it will last and what to expect, the easier it is to cope. For example, if you go into surgery with a realistic picture of what to expect post-op, a painful recovery will be less traumatic than if you were expecting to bounce back immediately.

Reaction Endeavour on Stress

As per famous Connie Lillas uses a driving analogy to describe the three most common ways people respond when they're overwhelmed by stress:

- **Foot on the gas :** An angry or agitated stress response. You're heated, keyed up, overly emotional, and unable to sit still.

Table 3.1. Which Enlighten Different Types of Stress

Cognitive Symptoms	Physical Symptoms
Memory problems Inability to concentrate Poor judgment Seeing only the negative Anxious or racing thoughts Constant worrying	Moodiness Irritability or short temper Agitation, inability to relax Feeling overwhelmed Sense of loneliness and isolation Depression or general unhappiness
Physical Symptoms	**Behavioural Symptoms**
Aches and pain Diarrhea or constipation Nausea, dizziness Chest pain, rapid heartbeat Loss of sex drive Frequent colds	Eating more or less Sleeping too much or too little Isolating yourself from others Procrastinating or neglecting responsibilities Using alcohol, cigarettes, or drugs to relax Nervous habits (e.g. nail biting, pacing)

- **Foot on the brake :** A withdrawn or depressed stress response. You shut down, space out, and show very little energy or emotion.
- **Foot on both :** A tense and frozen stress response. You "freeze" under pressure and can't do anything. You look paralyzed, but under the surface you're extremely agitated.

Keep in mind that the signs and symptoms of stress can also be caused by other psychological and medical problems. Doctor can help you determine whether or not your symptoms are stress-related.

Methods of Stress Management

Relaxation techniques are an essential part of your quest for stress management. Relaxation isn't just about peace of mind or enjoying a hobby. Relaxation is a process that decreases the wear and tear on your mind and body from the challenges and hassles of daily life. Whether your stress is spiraling out of control or you've already got it tamed, you can benefit from learning relaxation techniques. Learning basic relaxation techniques is easy, often free or low cost, and poses little risk. Explore these simple relaxation techniques to get you started on de-stressing your life and improving your health.

Benefits of Relaxation Techniques

Practising relaxation techniques can reduce stress symptoms by:

- Slowing your heart rate
- Lowering blood pressure
- Slowing your breathing rate
- Increasing blood flow to major muscles
- Reducing muscle tension and chronic pain
- Improving concentration
- Reducing anger and frustration
- Boosting confidence to handle problems

Some of the relaxation techniques as described below:

- **Autogenic relaxation :** Autogenic means something that comes from within you. In this relaxation technique, you use both visual imagery and body awareness to reduce stress. You repeat words or suggestions in your mind to help you relax and reduce muscle tension. You may imagine a peaceful place and then focus on controlled, relaxing breathing, slowing your heart rate, or feeling different physical sensations, such as relaxing each arm or leg one by one.
- **Progressive muscle relaxation :** In this relaxation technique, you focus on slowly tensing and then relaxing each muscle group. This helps you focus on the difference between muscle tension and relaxation. You become more aware of physical sensations. One method is to start by tensing and relaxing the muscles in your toes and progressively working your way up to your neck and head. Tense your muscles for at least five seconds and then relax for 30 seconds, and repeat.
- **Visualization :** In this relaxation technique, you form mental images to take a visual journey to a peaceful, calming place or situation. During visualization, try to use as many senses as you can, including smell, sight, sound and touch. If you imagine relaxing at the ocean, for instance, think about such things as the smell of salt water, the sound of crashing waves and the warmth of the sun on your body. You may want to close your eyes, sit in a quiet spot and loosen any tight clothing.

Identify Sources of Stress and Way to Manage

Stress management starts with identifying the sources of stress in your life. This isn't as easy as it sounds. Your true sources of stress aren't always obvious, and it's all too easy to overlook your own stress-inducing thoughts, feelings, and behaviors.

Identify your true sources of stress, look closely at your habits, attitude, and excuses:

- Do you explain away stress as temporary ("I just have a million things going on right now") even though you can't remember the last time you took a breather?
- Do you define stress as an integral part of your work or home life ("Things are always crazy around here") or as a part of your personality ("I have a lot of nervous energy, that's all").
- Do you blame your stress on other people or outside events, or view it as entirely normal and unexceptional?

Different Ways to Manage Stress

Strategies may temporarily reduce stress, but they cause more damage in the long run :

- Smoking
- Drinking too much
- Overeating or under eating
- Zoning out for hours in front of the TV or computer
- Withdrawing from friends, family, and activities
- Using pills or drugs to relax
- Sleeping too much
- Procrastinating
- Filling up every minute of the day to avoid facing problems
- Taking out your stress on others (lashing out, angry outbursts, physical violence).

Some of the tested way how to minimize the stress as mentioned below:

- **Learn how to say "no" :** Know your limits and stick to them. Whether in your personal or professional life, refuse to accept added responsibilities when you're close to reaching them. Taking on more than you can handle is a surefire recipe for stress.
- **Avoid people who stress you out :** If someone consistently causes stress in your life and you can't turn

the relationship around, limit the amount of time you spend with that person or end the relationship entirely.

- **Take control of your environment :** If the evening news makes you anxious, turn the TV off. If traffic's got you tense, take a longer but less-traveled route. If going to the market is an unpleasant chore, do your grocery shopping online.
- **Avoid hot-button topics :** If you get upset over religion or politics, cross them off your conversation list. If you repeatedly argue about the same subject with the same people, stop bringing it up or excuse yourself when it's the topic of discussion.
- **Pare down your to-do list :** Analyze your schedule, responsibilities, and daily tasks. If you've got too much on your plate, distinguish between the "shoulds" and the "musts." Drop tasks that aren't truly necessary to the bottom of the list or eliminate them entirely.
- **Express your feelings instead of bottling them up :** If something or someone is bothering you, communicate your concerns in an open and respectful way. If you don't voice your feelings, resentment will build and the situation will likely remain the same.
- **Be willing to compromise :** When you ask someone to change their behavior, be willing to do the same. If you both are willing to bend at least a little, you'll have a good chance of finding a happy middle ground.
- **Be more assertive :** Don't take a backseat in your own life. Deal with problems head on, doing your best to anticipate and prevent them. If you've got an exam to study for and your chatty roommate just got home, say up front that you only have five minutes to talk.
- **Manage your time better :** Poor time management can cause a lot of stress. When you're stretched too thin and running behind, it's hard to stay calm and focused. But if you plan ahead and make sure you don't overextend yourself, you can alter the amount of stress you're under.

- **Reframe problems :** Try to view stressful situations from a more positive perspective. Rather than fuming about a traffic jam, look at it as an opportunity to pause and regroup, listen to your favorite radio station, or enjoy some alone time.
- **Look at the big picture :** Take perspective of the stressful situation. Ask yourself how important it will be in the long run. Will it matter in a month? A year? Is it really worth getting upset over? If the answer is no, focus your time and energy elsewhere.
- **Adjust your standards :** Perfectionism is a major source of avoidable stress. Stop setting yourself up for failure by demanding perfection. Set reasonable standards for yourself and others, and learn to be okay with "good enough."
- **Focus on the positive :** When stress is getting you down, take a moment to reflect on all the things you appreciate in your life, including your own positive qualities and gifts. This simple strategy can help you keep things in perspective.
- **Don't try to control the uncontrollable :** Many things in life are beyond our control—particularly the behavior of other people. Rather than stressing out over them, focus on the things you can control such as the way you choose to react to problems.
- **Look for the upside :** As the saying goes, "What doesn't kill us makes us stronger." When facing major challenges, try to look at them as opportunities for personal growth. If your own poor choices contributed to a stressful situation, reflect on them and learn from your mistakes.
- **Share your feelings :** Talk to a trusted friend or make an appointment with a therapist. Expressing what you're going through can be very cathartic, even if there's nothing you can do to alter the stressful situation.

- **Learn to forgive :** Accept the fact that we live in an imperfect world and that people make mistakes. Let go of anger and resentments. Free yourself from negative energy by forgiving and moving on.
- **Set aside relaxation time :** Include rest and relaxation in your daily schedule. Don't allow other obligations to encroach. This is your time to take a break from all responsibilities and recharge your batteries.
- **Connect with others :** Spend time with positive people who enhance your life. A strong support system will buffer you from the negative effects of stress.
- **Do something you enjoy every day :** Make time for leisure activities that bring you joy, whether it be stargazing, playing the piano, or working on your bike.
- **Keep your sense of humor :** This includes the ability to laugh at yourself. The act of laughing helps your body fight stress in a number of ways.
- **Exercise regularly :** Physical activity plays a key role in reducing and preventing the effects of stress. Make time for at least 30 minutes of exercise, three times per week. Nothing beats aerobic exercise for releasing pent-up stress and tension.
- **Eat a healthy diet :** Well-nourished bodies are better prepared to cope with stress, so be mindful of what you eat. Start your day right with breakfast, and keep your energy up and your mind clear with balanced, nutritious meals throughout the day.
- **Reduce caffeine and sugar :** The temporary "highs" caffeine and sugar provide often end in with a crash in mood and energy. By reducing the amount of coffee, soft drinks, chocolate, and sugar snacks in your diet, you'll feel more relaxed and you'll sleep better.
- **Avoid alcohol, cigarettes, and drugs :** Self-medicating with alcohol or drugs may provide an easy escape from stress, but the relief is only temporary. Don't avoid or

mask the issue at hand; deal with problems head on and with a clear mind.

- **Get enough sleep** : Adequate sleep fuels your mind, *as* well as your body. Feeling tired will increase your stress because it may cause you to think irrationally.

Conclusion

All of us are under stress all of the time. Hans Selye refers to the "stress of life", meaning that life itself is stressful. Although we are constantly stressed, we are rarely consciously aware of it. Thus, it is not recognized as a potential killer of vitality, good health, and even life.

REFERENCES

Benefits of Meditation for Stress Management, By *Elizabeth Scott, M.S.,* Jan 22, 2010 National Statistics.

Stress-related and physiological disorders. Health & Safety Executive (HSE).

Guide to Surviving Working Life. Mind (National Association for Mental Health).

Relaxation Techniques for Stress Relief Management

—G. Chandrayya*

The body's natural relaxation response is a powerful antidote to stress. Relaxation techniques such as deep breathing, visualization, progressive muscle relaxation, meditation, and yoga can help you activate this relaxation response. When practiced regularly, these activities lead to a reduction in your everyday stress levels and a boost in your feelings of joy and serenity. What's more, they also serve a protective quality by teaching you how to stay calm and collected in the face of life's curveballs.

The Relaxation Response

You can't avoid all stress, but you can counteract its negative effects by learning how to evoke the *relaxation response,* a state of deep rest that is the polar opposite of the stress response.

The stress response floods your body with chemicals that prepare you for "fight or flight." But while the stress response is helpful in true emergency situations where you must be alert, it wears your body down when constantly activated.

The relaxation response brings your system back into balance : deepening your breathing, reducing stress hormones, slowing down your heart rate and blood pressure, and relaxing your muscles.

In addition to its calming physical effects, research shows that the relaxation response also increases energy and focus,

* Senior Faculty, Deptt. of Commerce Government College (A), Rajahmundry, E.G. Dist., A.P.

combats illness, relieves aches and pains, heightens problem-solving abilities, and boosts motivation and productivity. Best of all - with a little practice - anyone can reap these benefits.

Starting a Relaxation Practice

A variety of relaxation techniques help you achieve the relaxation response. Those whose stress-busting benefits have been widely studied include deep breathing, progressive muscle relaxation, meditation, visualization, *yoga*, and *tai chi*.

Learning the basics of these relaxation techniques isn't difficult. But it takes practice to truly harness their stress-relieving power : daily practice, in fact. Most stress experts recommend setting aside at least 10 to 20 minutes a day for your relaxation practice. If you'd like to get even more stress relief, aim for 30 minutes to an hour.

Getting the Most Out of Your Relaxation Practice

- **Set aside time in your daily schedule :** The best way to start and maintain a relaxation practice is by incorporating it into your daily routine. Schedule a set time either once or twice a day for your practice. You may find that it's easier to stick with your practice if you do it first thing in the morning, before other tasks and responsibilities get in the way.
- **Don't practice when you're sleepy :** These techniques can relax you so much that they can make you very sleepy, especially if it's close to bedtime. You will get the most out of these techniques if you practice when you're fully awake and alert.
- **Choose a technique that appeals to you :** There is no single relaxation technique that is best. When choosing a relaxation technique, consider your specific needs, preferences, and fitness level. The right relaxation technique is the one that resonates with you and fits your lifestyle.
- **Deep breathing for stress relief :** With its focus on full, cleansing breaths, deep breathing is a simple, yet

powerful, relaxation technique. It's easy to learn, can be practiced almost anywhere, and provides a quick way to get your stress levels in check. Deep breathing is the cornerstone of many other relaxation practices, too, and can be combined with other relaxing elements such as aromatherapy and music. All you really need is a few minutes and a place to stretch out.

How to Practice Deep Breathing

The key to deep breathing is to breathe deeply from the abdomen, getting as much fresh air as possible in your lungs. When you take deep breaths from the abdomen, rather than shallow breaths from your upper chest, you inhale more oxygen. The more oxygen you get, the less tense, short of breath, and anxious you feel. So the next time you feel stressed, take a minute to slow down and breathe deeply:

- Sit comfortably with your back straight. Put one hand on your chest and the other on your stomach.
- Breathe in through your nose. The hand on your stomach should rise. The hand on your chest should move very little.
- Exhale through your mouth, pushing out as much air as you can while contracting your abdominal muscles. The hand on your stomach should move in as you exhale, but your other hand should move very little.
- Continue to breathe in through your nose and out through your mouth. Try to inhale enough so that your lower abdomen rises and falls. Count slowly as you exhale.

If you have a hard time breathing from your abdomen while sitting up, try lying on the floor. Put a small book on your stomach, and try to breathe so that the book rises as you inhale and falls as you exhale.

Progressive Muscle Relaxation for Stress Relief

Progressive muscle relaxation is another effective and widely used strategy for stress relief. It involves a two-step process in which you systematically tense and relax different muscle groups in the body.

With regular practice, progressive muscle relaxation gives you an intimate familiarity with what tension—as well as complete relaxation—feels like in different parts of the body. This awareness helps you spot and counteract the first signs of the muscular tension that accompanies stress. And as your body relaxes, so will your mind. You can combine deep breathing with progressive muscle relaxation for an additional level of relief from stress.

Progressive Muscle Relaxation Sequence

- Right foot
- Left foot
- Right calf
- Left calf
- Right thigh
- Left thigh
- Hips and buttocks
- Stomach
- Chest
- Back
- Right arm and hand
- Left arm and hand
- Neck and shoulders
- Face

Most progressive muscle relaxation practitioners start at the feet and work their way up to the face. For a sequence of muscle groups to follow, see the box to the right:

- Loosen your clothing, take off your shoes, and get comfortable.
- Take a few minutes to relax, breathing in and out in slow, deep breaths.

- When you're relaxed and ready to start, shift your attention to your right foot. Take a moment to focus on the way it feels.
- Slowly tense the muscles in your right foot, squeezing as tightly as you can. Hold for a count of 10.
- Relax your right foot. Focus on the tension flowing away and the way your foot feels as it becomes limp and loose.
- Stay in this relaxed state for a moment, breathing deeply and slowly.
- When you're ready, shift your attention to your left foot. Follow the same sequence of muscle tension and release.
- Move slowly up through your body—legs, abdomen, back, neck, face—contracting and relaxing the muscle groups as you go.

Mindfulness Meditation for Stress Relief

Meditation that cultivates *mindfulness* is particularly effective at reducing stress, anxiety, depression, and other negative emotions. Mindfulness is the quality of being fully engaged in the present moment, without analyzing or otherwise "over-thinking" the experience. Rather than worrying about the future or dwelling on the past, mindfulness meditation switches the focus to what's happening right now.

For stress relief, try the following mindfulness meditation techniques:

- **Body scan** : Body scanning cultivates mindfulness by focusing your attention on various parts of your body. Like progressive muscle relaxation, you start with your feet and work your way up. However, instead of tensing and relaxing your muscles, you simply focus on the way each part of your body feels without labeling the sensations as either "good" or "bad".
- **Walking meditation** : You don't have to be seated or still to meditate. In walking meditation, mindfulness

involves being focused on the physicality of each step — the sensation of your feet touching the ground, the rhythm of your breath while moving, and feeling the wind against your face.

- **Mindful eating** : If you reach for food when you're under stress or gulp your meals down in a rush, try eating mindfully. Sit down at the table and focus your full attention on the meal (no TV, newspapers, or eating on the run). Eat slowly, taking the time to fully enjoy and concentrate on each bite.

Mindfulness meditation is not equal to zoning out. It takes effort to maintain your concentration and to bring it back to the present moment when your mind wanders or you start to drift off. But with regular practice, mindfulness meditation actually changes the brain-strengthening the areas associated with joy and relaxation, and weakening those involved in negativity and stress.

Starting a Meditation Practice

All you need to start meditating are :

- **A quiet environment** : Choose a secluded place in your home, office, garden, place of worship, or in the great outdoors where you can relax without distractions or interruptions.
- **A comfortable position** : Get comfortable, but avoid lying down as this may lead to you falling asleep. Sit up with your spine straight, either in a chair or on the floor. You can also try a cross-legged or lotus position.
- **A point of focus** : Pick a meaningful word or phrase and repeat it throughout your session. You may also choose to focus on an object in your surroundings to enhance your concentration, or alternately, you can close your eyes.
- **An observant, noncritical attitude** : Don't worry about distracting thoughts that go through your mind or about

how well you're doing. If thoughts intrude during your relaxation session, don't fight them. Instead, gently turn your attention back to your point of focus.

Guided Imagery for Stress Relief

Visualization, or *guided imagery, is* a variation on traditional meditation that can help relieve stress. When used as a relaxation technique, guided imagery involves imagining a scene in which you feel at peace, free to let go of all tension and anxiety. Choose whatever setting is most calming to you, whether a tropical beach, a favorite childhood spot, or a quiet wooded glen. You can do this visualization exercise on your own, with a therapist's help, or using an audio recording.

Close your eyes and let your worries drift away. Imagine your restful place. Picture it as vividly as you can—everything you can see, hear, smell, and feel. Guided imagery works best if you incorporate as many sensory details as possible. For example, if you are thinking about a dock on a quiet lake:

- See the sun setting over the water
- Hear the birds singing
- Smell the pine trees
- Feel the cool water on your bare feet
- Taste the fresh, clean air

Yoga for Stress Relief

Yoga is an excellent stress relief technique. It involves a series of both moving and stationary poses, combined with deep breathing. The physical and mental benefits of yoga provide a natural counterbalance to stress, and strengthen the relaxation response in your daily life.

What Type of Yoga is Best for Stress?

Although almost all yoga classes end in a relaxation pose, classes that emphasize slow, steady movement and gentle stretching are best for stress relief. Look for labels like *gentle, for stress relief, or for beginners.* Power yoga, with its intense poses and focus on fitness, is not the best choice. If you're unsure whether a specific yoga class is appropriate for stress relief, call the studio or ask the teacher.

Since injuries can happen when yoga is practiced incorrectly, it's best to learn by attending group classes or hiring a private teacher. Once you've learned the basics, you can practice alone or with others, tailoring your practice as you see fit.

Tips for Starting a Yoga Practice

- **Consider your fitness level and any medical issues before joining a yoga class** : There are many yoga classes for different needs, such as prenatal yoga, yoga for seniors, and adaptive yoga (modified yoga for disabilities). "Hot" or Bikram yoga, which is practiced in a heated environment, might be too much if you are just starting out.
- **Look for a low-pressure environment where you can learn at your own pace** : Don't extend yourself beyond what feels comfortable, and always back off of a pose at the first sign of pain. A good teacher can show you alternate poses for ones that are too challenging for your health or fitness level.
- Click here for a searchable, international directory of yoga classes, provided by Yoga Finder. You can also look for yoga classes at local gyms and specialized yoga studios. Community centers or community colleges often offer yoga classes at discounted prices.

Tai chi for Stress Relief

If you've ever seen a group of people in the park slowly moving in synch, you've probably witnessed tai chi. Tai chi is a self-paced, non-competitive series of slow, flowing body movements. These movements emphasize concentration, relaxation, and the conscious circulation of vital energy throughout the body. Though tai chi has its roots in martial arts, today it is primarily practiced as a way of calming the mind, conditioning the body, and reducing stress. As in meditation, *tai chi* practitioners focus on their breathing and keeping their attention in the present moment.

Tai chi is a safe, low-impact option for people of all ages and levels of fitness, including older adults and those recovering from injuries. Once you've learned the moves, you can practice it anywhere, at any time, by yourself, or with others.

Making Tai Chi Work for You

- As with yoga, *tai chi* is best learned in a class or from a private instructor.
- Although tai chi is normally very safe and gentle, be sure to discuss any health or mobility concerns with your instructor.
- Tai chi classes are often offered in community centers, senior centers, or local community colleges.
- Click here to find a qualified instructor recommended by the *Tai Chi* Network.

Massage Therapy for Stress Relief

Getting a massage provides deep relaxation, and as the muscles in your body relax, so does your overstressed mind. And you don't have to visit the spa to enjoy the benefits of massage. There are many simple self-massage techniques you can use to relax and release stress.

Self-Massage Techniques

Source: Northwestern Health Sciences University

Scalp Soother	Place your thumbs behind your ears while spreading your fingers on top of your head. Move your scalp back

	and forth slightly by making circles with your fingertips for 15-20 seconds.
Easy on the Eyes	Close your eyes and place your ring fingers directly under your eyebrows, near the bridge of your nose. Slowly increase the pressure for 5-10 seconds, then gently release. Repeat 2-3 times.
Sinus Pressure Relief	Place your fingertips at the bridge of your nose. Slowly slide your fingers down your nose and across the top of your cheekbones to the outside of your eyes.
Shoulder Tension Relief	Reach one arm across the front of your body to your opposite shoulder. Using a circular motion, press firmly on the muscle above your shoulder blade. Repeat on the other side.

The most common type of massage is Swedish massage, a soothing technique specifically designed to relax and energize. Another common type of massage is Shiatsu, also known as acupressure. In Shiatsu massage, therapists use their fingers to manipulate the body's pressure points.

Although self-massage is good for stress relief, getting a massage from a professional massage therapist can be tremendously relaxing and more through then what you can do yourself. When booking a massage, try types like Swedish or Shiatsu, which promote overall relaxation. Deep tissue and sports massages are more aggressive. They often target specific areas and may leave you sore for a couple of days, making them less effective for relaxation and stress relief.

- The American Massage Therapy Association provides an online directory of massage therapists.
- If you are on a budget, look around for massage schools. They often provide massages at reduced prices while training students.

UNDERSTANDING STRESS

Signs, Symptoms, Causes, and Effects

Modern life is full of hassles, deadlines, frustrations, and demands. For many people, stress is so commonplace that it has become a way of life. Stress isn't always bad. In small doses, it can help you perform under pressure and motivate you to do your best. But when you're constantly running in emergency mode, your mind and body pay the price.

If you frequently find yourself feeling frazzled and overwhelmed, it's time to take action to bring your nervous system back into balance. You can protect yourself by learning how to recognize the signs and symptoms of stress and taking steps to reduce its harmful effects.

This article includes the following:

- What is stress?
- Effects of chronic stress
- How much stress is too much?
- Causes of stress
- Signs and symptoms of stress overload
- Dealing with stress
- Related links for stress

WHAT IS STRESS?

The Body's Stress Response

When you perceive a threat, your nervous system responds by releasing a flood of stress hormones, including adrenaline and cortisol. These hormones rouse the body for emergency action.

Your heart pounds faster, muscles tighten, blood pressure rises, breath quickens, and your senses become sharper. These physical changes increase your strength and stamina, speed your reaction time, and enhance your focus-preparing you to either fight or flee from the danger at hand.

Stress is a normal physical response to events that make you feel threatened or upset your balance in some way. When you sense danger - whether it's real or imagined - the body's defenses kick into high gear in a rapid, automatic process known as the "fight-or-flight" reaction, or the *stress response.*

The stress response is the body's way of protecting you. When working properly, it helps you stay focused, energetic, and alert. In emergency situations, stress can save your life-giving you extra strength to defend yourself, for example, or spurring you to slam on the brakes to avoid an accident.

The stress response also helps you rise to meet challenges. Stress is what keeps you on your toes during a presentation at work, sharpens your concentration when you're attempting the game-winning free throw, or drives you to study for an exam when you'd rather be watching TV.

But beyond a certain point, stress stops being helpful and starts causing major damage to your health, your mood, your productivity, your relationships, and your quality of life.

EFFECTS OF CHRONIC STRESS

The body doesn't distinguish between physical and psychological threats. When you're stressed over a busy schedule, an argument with a friend, a traffic jam, or a mountain of bills, your body reacts just as strongly as if you were facing a life-or-death situation. If you have a lot of responsibilities and worries, your emergency stress response may be "on" most of the time. The more your body's stress system is activated, the easier it is to trip and the harder it is to shut off.

Long-term exposure to stress can lead to serious health problems. Chronic stress disrupts nearly 'every system in your body. It can raise blood pressure, suppress the immune system, increase the risk of heart attack and stroke, contribute to infertility, and speed up the aging process. Long-term stress can even rewire the brain, leaving you more vulnerable to anxiety and depression.

Many Health Problems are Caused or Exacerbated by Stress, Including

- Pain of any kind
- Depression
- Heart disease
- Obesity
- Digestive problems
- Autoimmune diseases
- Sleep problems
- Skin conditions, such as eczema.

HOW MUCH STRESS IS TOO MUCH?

Because of the widespread damage stress can cause, it's important to know your own limit. But just how much stress is "too much" differs from person to person. Some people roll with the punches, while others crumble at the slightest obstacle or frustration. Some people even seem to thrive on the excitement and challenge of a high-stress lifestyle.

Your ability to tolerate stress depends on many factors, including the quality of your relationships, your general outlook on life, your emotional intelligence, and genetics.

Things that Influence Your Stress Tolerance Level

- **Your support network :** A strong network of supportive friends and family members is an enormous buffer against life's stressors. On the flip side, the more lonely and isolated you are, the greater your vulnerability to stress.

- **Your sense of control :** If you have confidence in yourself and your ability to influence events and persevere through challenges, it's easier to take stress in stride. People who are vulnerable to stress tend to feel like things are out of their control.
- **Your attitude and outlook :** Stress-hardy people have an optimistic attitude. They tend to embrace challenges, have a strong sense of humor, accept that change is a part of life, and believe in a higher power or purpose.
- **Your ability to deal with your emotions :** You're extremely vulnerable to stress if you don't know how to calm and soothe yourself-when you're feeling sad, angry, or afraid. The ability to bring your emotions into balance helps you bounce back from adversity.
- **Your knowledge and preparation :** The more you know about a stressful situation, including how long it will last and what to expect, the easier it is to cope. For example, if you go into surgery with a realistic picture of what to expect post-op, a painful recovery will be less traumatic than if you were expecting to bounce back immediately.

Am I in Control of Stress or is Stress Controlling me?

- When I feel agitated, do I know how to quickly calm and soothe myself?
- Can I easily let go of my anger?
- Can I turn to others at work to help me calm down and feel better?
- When I come home at night, do I walk in the door feeling alert and relaxed?
- Am I seldom distracted or moody?
- Am I able to recognize upsets that others seem to be experiencing?
- Do I easily turn to friends or family members for a calming influence?
- When my energy is low, do I know how to boost it?

CAUSES OF STRESS

Top Ten Stressful Life Events

1. Spouse's death
2. Divorce
3. Marriage separation
4. Jail term
5. Death of a close relative
6. Injury or illness
7. Marriage
8. Fired from job
9. Marriage reconciliation
10. Retirement.

The situations and pressures that cause stress are known as stressors. We usually think of stressors as being negative, such as an exhausting work schedule or a rocky relationship.

However, anything that puts high demands on you or forces you to adjust can be stressful. This includes positive events such as getting married, buying a house, going to college, or receiving a promotion.

What causes stress depends, at least in part, on your perception of it. Something that's stressful to you may not faze someone else; they may even enjoy it.

For example, your morning commute may make you anxious and tense because you worry that traffic will make you late. Others, however, may find the trip relaxing because they allow more than enough time and enjoy listening to music while they drive.

Common External Causes of Stress

Not all stress is caused by external factors. Stress can also be self-generated:

- Major life changes
- Financial problems

- Work
- Being too busy
- Relationship difficulties
- Children and family

Common Internal Causes of Stress

Not all stress is caused by external factors. Stress can also be self-generated:

- Inability to accept uncertainty
- Unrealistic expectations
- Pessimism
- Perfectionism
- Negative self-talk
- Lack of assertiveness

What's Stressful For You?

What's stressful for you may be quite different from what's stressful to. your best friend, your spouse, or the person next door. For example:

- Some people enjoy speaking in public; others are terrified.
- Some people are more productive under deadline pressure; others are miserably tense.
- Some people are eager to help family and friends through difficult times; others find it very stressful.
- Some people feel comfortable complaining about bad service in a restaurant; others find it so difficult to complain that they prefer to suffer in silence.
- Some people may feel that changes at work represent a welcome opportunity; others worry about whether they'll be able to cope.

SIGNS AND SYMPTOMS OF STRESS OVERLOAD

It's important to learn how to recognize when your stress levels are out of control. The most dangerous thing about stress is how easily it can creep up on you. You get used to it. It starts to feels familiar - even normal. You don't notice how much it's affecting you, even as it takes a heavy toll.

The signs and symptoms of stress overload can be almost anything. Stress affects the mind, body, and behavior in many ways, and everyone experiences stress differently.

How do You Respond to Stress?

Psychologist Connie Lillas uses a driving analogy to describe the three most common ways people respond when they're overwhelmed by stress:

- **Foot on the gas :** An angry or agitated stress response. You're heated, keyed up, overly emotional, and unable to sit still.
- **Foot on the brake :** A withdrawn or depressed stress response. You shut down, space out, and show very little energy or emotion.
- **Foot on both :** A tense and frozen stress response. You "freeze" under pressure and can't do anything. You look paralyzed, but under the surface you're extremely agitated.

The following table lists some of the common warning signs and symptoms of stress. The more signs and symptoms you notice in yourself, the closer you may be to stress overload.

STRESS WARNING SIGNS AND SYMPTOMS

Cognitive Symptoms

- Memory problems
- Inability to concentrate
- Poor judgment
- Seeing only the negative

- Anxious or racing thoughts
- Constant worrying

Physical Symptoms

- Aches and pains
- Diarrhea or constipation
- Nausea, dizziness
- Chest pain, rapid heartbeat
- Loss of sex drive
- Frequent colds

Emotional Symptoms

- Moodiness
- Irritability or short temper
- Agitation, inability to relax
- Feeling overwhelmed
- Sense of loneliness and isolation
- Depression or general unhappiness

Behavioural Symptoms

- Eating more or less
- Sleeping too much or too little
- Isolating yourself from others
- Procrastinating or neglecting responsibilities
- Using alcohol, cigarettes, or drugs to relax
- Nervous habits (e.g. nail biting, pacing)

Keep in mind that the signs and symptoms of stress can also be caused by other psychological and medical problems. If you're experiencing any of the warning signs of stress, it's important to see a doctor for a full evaluation. Your doctor can help you determine whether or not your symptoms are stress-related.

DEALING WITH STRESS AND ITS SYMPTOMS

While unchecked stress is undeniably damaging, there are many things you can do to reduce its impact and cope with symptoms.

Learn How to Manage Stress

You may feel like the stress in your life is out of your control, but you can always control the way you respond. Managing stress is all about taking charge : taking charge of your thoughts, your emotions, your schedule, your environment, and the way you deal with problems. Stress management involves changing the stressful situation when you can, changing your reaction when you can't, taking care of yourself, and making time for rest and relaxation.

Read Stress Management : How to Reduce, Prevent, and Cope with Stress.

Strengthen your Relationships

A strong support network is your greatest protection against stress. When you have trusted friends and family members you know you can count on, life's pressures don't seem as overwhelming. So spend time with the people you love and don't let your responsibilities keep you from having a social life. If you don't have any close relationships, or your relationships are the source of your stress, make it a priority to build stronger and more satisfying connections.

Tips for reaching out and building relationships :

- Help someone else by volunteering.
- Go for a walk with a workout buddy.
- Have lunch or coffee with a co-worker.
- Schedule a weekly dinner date
- Call or email an old friend.
- Take a class or join a club.

Read Relationship Help : Building Great Relationships Using Emotional Intelligence.

LEARN HOW TO RELAX

You can't completely eliminate stress from your life, but you can control how much.it affects you. Relaxation techniques such as yoga, meditation, and deep breathing activate the body's relaxation response, a state of restfulness that is the opposite of the stress response. When practiced regularly, these activities lead to a reduction in your everyday stress levels and a boost in your feelings of joy and serenity. They also increase your ability to stay calm and collected under pressure.

Read Relaxation Techniques for Stress Relief : Relaxation Exercises to Reduce Stress, Anxiety, and Depression.

Invest in Your Emotional Health

Most people ignore their emotional health until there's a problem. But just as it requires time and energy to build or maintain your physical health, so it is with your emotional well-being. The more you put in to it, the stronger it will be. People with good emotional health have an ability to bounce back from stress and adversity. This ability is called resilience. They remain focused, flexible, and positive in bad times as well as good. The good news is that there are many steps you can take to build your resilience and your overall emotional health.

Stress can be Defined as:

'The way your body responds to the demands of your life style' i.e., the effects of wear and tear on your body. Most people think of stress as a mental state but it is in fact, very largely, a physical condition. When a person is subjected to a stress-producing effect known as stressor (a challenge, pressure, stimulus, external influence, etc.) it is registered in the brain. The brain gives various parts of the body instructions for a chain of reactions known as stress reaction or stress response. Different People can tolerate different levels of stress, Each person needs

to work on their own stress control techniques according to their tolerance levels. Here are the first steps towards greater awareness of stress levels:

- How does stress affect you?
- Which stressors affect you particularly?
- How can you be more aware o your stress response?
- What is the strength and duration of your stress response?
- Which stress management techniques most suit you?

Effect of Stress

Stress response : The stress response can be described as a chain of reaction of changes within the body:

- Shallower, quicker breathing,
- Faster heart beat,
- Rise in blood pressure,
- Reduction in the blood supply to hands and feet,
- Increase in body's metabolism,
- Faster clotting of blood,
- Increased blood flow to the muscles,
- Reduction of blood supply to stomach and abdomen,
- Tensing of muscles,
- Sharpening of all senses,
- Reduction of tension in bowels and stomach functions,
- Reduction in the efficiency of the immune system.

Of course all these changes in the body also have an effect on the brain and this can cause an alert mental state, leading to:

- Faster activity of brain,
- Improvement of short term judgement,
- Faster decision making,

- Improved memory powers,
- Sharper focusing of the attention.

Positive Effects of Stress

Stress is valuable under certain circumstances, e.g. sports, making speeches and taking examinations. The stress response puts people on their mettle, increase alertness, improves sight, strengthens muscles and reduces reaction times. The stress response increases our ability to stand and fight or turn and flee and to mobilize all our resources to achieve whatever we decide to do. Another positive is the zest that stress adds to life by stimulating the stress and the passions. Many people need challenge in their lives and would be unhappy without it. Stress only has a positive effect if it is not allowed to build up or feed on itself, i.e. if it can be worked off.

Negative Effects of Stress

The negative effects of stress show particularly when a person allows stress to remain in the body, usually when a person allows stress to remain in the body, usually when there is no chance to take the necessary steps to release a stress response that is too strong or lasts too long. The negative effects of stress show up in three ways in particular:

1. Unsuitable behaviour
2. Lower energy and performance levels
3. Poorer health

Here are some examples of the negative effects of stress:

Unsuitable behaviour

- Loser behaviour
- Short temper
- Bad smoking, eating and drinking habits
- More frequent mistakes
- Less flexibility

Lower energy and performance levels

- Reduced concentration
- Increased forgetfulness
- Poor judgement
- Prone to feeling of tiredness

Poorer to health

- Heart and circulatory diseases
- Ulcers
- Infectious diseases
- Skin diseases

Stressors

The first step in learning to control your stress, and live with it, is to find out what your stresses are, i.e. what stresses you personally. Stressors are divided into physical and social groupings and the social stresses can be subdivided into further:

Physical Stressors

Example:

- Heat, Fire, Traffic, Violence, Own Illness,
- Cold,
- Noise,
- Poor working conditions and equipment.

Social Stressors

There are four main causes of social stress:

Social, Economic and Political

- Unemployment
- Inflation
- Cost of housing

- Taxes
- Crime
- Pollution
- Technological change.

Family

- Sharing of workload
- Jealousy
- Sex roles
- Different values
- Death or illness in the family
- Different lifestyle,
- Money problems.

Job and Career

- Deadlines
- Muddled communication
- Traveling time
- Interruptions
- Competition
- Power struggles
- Education/Training.

Interpersonal and Environmental

- Different values
- Obligations
- Waiting time
- Poor service
- Smokers/Non-smokers
- Driving habits
- Social expectations

Stress Signals (Do not Treat the Symptoms, Treat the Cause)

Examples of stress signals:

Physical

- Changes in breathing rhythm
- Tense and aching muscles
- Headaches
- Sweating
- Cold hands and feets
- Changes in appetite
- Stomach problems, heartburn

Mental

- Lack of concentration
- More frequent mistakes
- Forgetfulness/Absentmindedness
- Tendency to over-react
- Poorer judgement

Emotional

- Irritation/Short Temper
- Nervousness
- Depression/Silence
- Emotional outbursts/Crying

Behavioral

- Insomnia
- Increased drinking and smoking
- Absenteeism
- Clumsiness

Ways of Managing Stress

1. Awareness of stress
2. Analysis and treatment of the actual stressor :
   (*i*) Take action
   (*ii*) Withdraw
   (*iii*) Do Nothing
   (*iv*) Adjust your attitude
3. Physical Fitness
4. A healthy diet
5. Relaxation
6. Take short rest breaks during the day.

Breathing

Take five completely relaxed breaths feeling your stomach moving and your stomach muscles relaxing.

Breath 1 : Breathe in deeply and out again fully.

For the next four breaths tense a group of muscles as you breathe in and relax them as you breathe out.

Breath 2 : Feet.

Breath 3 : Hands and upper part of body.

Breath 4 : Jaw.

Breath 5 : Stomach.

What is Stress?

Stress is the "wear and tear" our bodies experience as we adjust to our continually changing environment; it has physical and emotional effects on us. and can create positive or negative feelings. As a positive influence, stress can help compel us to action; it can result in a new awareness and an exciting new perspective. As a negative influence, it can result in feelings of distrust, rejection, anger, and depression, which in turn can lead to health problems such as headaches, upset stomach, rashes, insomnia, ulcers, high blood pressure, heart disease, and stroke. With the death of a loved one, the birth of a child, a job promotion, or a new relationship, we experience stress as we readjust our lives. In so adjusting to different circumstances, stress will help or hinder us depending on how we react to it.

How Can I Eliminate Stress From My Life?

As we have seen, positive stress adds anticipation and excitement to life, and we all thrive under a certain amount of stress. Deadlines, competitions, confrontations, and even our frustrations and sorrows add depth and enrichment to our lives. Our goal is not to eliminate stress but to learn how to manage it and how to use it to help us. Insufficient stress acts as a depressant and may leave us feeling bored or dejected; on the other hand, excessive stress may leave us feeling "tied up in knots". What we need to do is find the optimal level of stress which will individually motivate but not overwhelm each of us.

How Can I Tell What is Optimal Stress For Me?

There is no single level of stress that is optimal for all people. We are all individual creatures with unique requirements. As such, what is distressing to one may be a joy to another. And even when we agree that a particular event is distressing, we are likely to differ in our physiological and psychological responses to it.

The person who loves to arbitrate disputes and move from job site to job site would be stressed in a job which was stable and routine, whereas the person who thrives under stable conditions would very likely be stressed in a job where duties were highly varied. Also, our personal stress requirements and the amount which we can tolerate before we become distressed changes with our life-styles and our ages.

It has been found that most illness is related to unrelieved stress. If you are experiencing stress symptoms, you have gone beyond your optimal stress level; you need to reduce the stress in your life and/or improve your ability to manage it.

How Can I Manage Stress Better?

Identifying unrelieved stress and being aware of its effect on our lives is not sufficient for reducing its harmful effects. Just as there are many sources of stress, there are many possibilities for its management. However, all require effort toward change: changing the source of stress and/or changing your reaction to it. How do you proceed?

Become Aware of your Stressors and your Emotional and Physical Reactions

- Notice your distress. Don't ignore it. Don't gloss over your problems.
- Determine what events distress you. What are you telling yourself about the meaning of these events?
- Determine how your body responds to the stress. Do you become nervous or physically upset? If so, in what specific ways?

Recognise What you can Change

- Can you change your stressors by avoiding or eliminating them completely?
- Can you reduce their intensity (manage them over a period of time instead of on a daily or weekly basis)?
- Can you shorten your exposure to stress (take a break, leave the physical premises)?
- Can you devote the time and energy necessary to making a change (goal setting, time management techniques, and delayed gratification strategies may be helpful here)?

Reduce the Intensity of your Emotional Reactions to Stress

- The stress reaction is triggered by your perception of danger, whether from a physical or emotional threat.

Are you viewing your stressors in exaggerated terms and viewing a difficult situation as a disaster?

- Are you expecting to please everyone?
- Are you overreacting and viewing things as absolutely critical and urgent? Do you feel you must always prevail in every situation?
- Work at adopting more moderate views; try to see the stress as something you can cope with rather than something that overpowers you.
- Try to temper your excess emotions. Put the situation in perspective. Do not labour on the negative aspects and the "what if's".

Learn to Notice and Moderate your Physical Reactions to Stress

- Slow, deep breathing will bring your heart rate and respiration back to normal.
- Relaxation techniques can reduce muscle tension. Electronic biofeedback can help you gain voluntary control over such things as muscle tension, heart rate, and blood pressure.
- Medications, when prescribed by a physician, can help in the short term in moderating your physical reactions. However, they alone are not the answer. Learning to moderate these reactions on your own is a preferable long-term solution.

Build your Physical Reserves

- Exercise for cardiovascular fitness three to four times a week (moderate, prolonged rhythmic exercise is best, such as walking, swimming, cycling, or jogging).
- Eat well-balanced, nutritious meals.
- Maintain your ideal weight.
- Avoid nicotine, excessive caffeine, and other stimulants.

- Mix leisure with work. Take breaks and get away when you can.
- Get enough sleep. Be as consistent with your sleep schedule as possible.

Maintain your Emotional Reserves

- Develop some mutually supportive friendships/ relationships.
- Pursue realistic goals which are meaningful to you, rather than goals others have for you that you do not share.
- Expect some frustrations, failures, and sorrows.
- Always be kind and gentle with yourself - be a friend to yourself.

Stress Management Techniques, Stress Reduction and Relief

—*Rookesh Kumar Misra**

Introduction

Employers should provide a stress-free work environment:, recognize where stress is becoming a problem for staff, and take action to reduce stress. Stress in the workplace reduces productivity, increases management pressures, and makes people ill in many ways, evidence of which is still increasing. Workplace stress affects the performance of the brain, including functions of work performance; memory, concentration, and learning. In the U.K. over 13 million working days are lost every year because of stress. Stress is believed to trigger 70 per cent of visits to doctors, and 85 per cent of serious illnesses (UK-HSE stress statistics). Stress at work also provides a serious risk of litigation for all employers and organisations, carrying significant liabilities for damages, bad publicity and loss of reputation. Dealing with stress-related claims also consumes vast amounts of management time. So, there are clearly strong economic and financial reasons for organisations to manage and reduce stress at wprk, aside from the obvious humanitarian and ethical considerations. If you are suffering from stress yourself the stress management guidelines here are just as relevant.

Quick Stress Reduction Techniques

If you are stressed, do one or all of these things, in whatever

* HR Manager, Hyderabad.

order that takes your fancy. These ideas can also be adapted for team development exercises.

The key to de-stressing in the moment is getting away from or removing yourself from the stressor. *Developing new habits* which regularly *remove you and distract you from stressors* and stressful situations and pressure is essentially how to manage stress on a more permanent basis.

In this modern world it is difficult if not impossible to change stressful situations. What we can do however is change and reduce our exposure to those stressful situations.

These stress reduction ideas and techniques are based on that simple principle. These tips won't change the situation causing the stress, but they will, more importantly, enable you to change your reaction and relationship to the stressful situations. And in keeping with the tone of this stress tips section, and since colour is regarded by many as a factor in affecting mood, the calming shade of green is used for the headings.

Humour

Humour is one of the greatest and quickest devices for reducing stress. Humour works because laughter produces helpful chemicals in the brain. Humour also gets your brain thinking and working in a different way - it distracts you from having a stressed mindset. Distraction is a simple effective de-stressor - it takes your thoughts away from the stress, and thereby diffuses the stressful feelings.Therefore most people will feel quite different and notice a change in mindset after laughing and being distracted by something humorous. Go read the *funny family fortunes answers.* Or try the *funny letters to the council.* Even if you've seen them a hundred times before. As you start to smile and chuckle the stress begins to dissipate. If this material fails to make you laugh then find something which does. Keep taking the laughter medicine until you feel suitably relaxed and re-charged.

Walk and Self-talk

You can extend the exercise by going to a park and jogging a little.Or do a few star-jumps - something energetic to get your body moving and relaxing. Or stroke a dog, or pick up some litter, or kick a kid's football. You can of course use other mantras or chants, depending on what you want to do and how far you want to get away from the stress causes.

Rehydrate

Most of us fail to drink enough water - that's water - not tea, coffee, coke, 'sports' drinks, Red Bull or fruit juice. . .

All of your organs, including your brain, are strongly dependent on water to function properly. It's how we are built.

If you starve your body of water you will function below your best - and you will get stressed. Physically and mentally.

Offices and workplaces commonly have a very dry atmosphere due to air conditioning, etc., which increases people's susceptibility to de-hydration.

This is why you must keep your body properly hydrated by regularly drinking water (most people need 4-8 glasses of water a day).

You will Drink more Water if you keep some on your Desk at All Times - It's Human Nature to Drink it if it's there - So go get Some Now

When you drink water you need to pee. This gives you a bit of a break and a bit of exercise now and then, which also reduces stress.

When you pee you can see if your body is properly hydrated (your pee will be clear or near clear - if it's yellow you are not taking enough water).

This will also prompt some amusing discussion and chuckling with your colleagues ("Nature calls - I'm off to the bog again. . .") which is also good for reducing stress.

You do not need to buy expensive mineral water. Tap water is fine.'

If you do not like the taste of tap water it's probably because of the chlorine (aquarium fish don't like it either), however the chlorine dissipates quite naturally after a few hours - even through a plastic bottle - so keep some ordinary tap water in the fridge for 2-3 hours and try it then.

If you want to be really exotic add a slice of lemon or lime. Kiwi and sharon fruit are nice too...

So now you are fully watered and guffawing and exercised up to the max, read on for ideas for how to prevent stress as well as reduce and manage it.

Catnap or Powernap

It's obviously essential if you are driving while tired, but a quick sleep is a powerful destressor too.

A lunchtime snooze is very practical for home-workers - it just requires the realisation that doing so is acceptable and beneficial (when we are conditioned unfortunately to think that sleeping during the day is lazy, rather than healthy).

At some stage conventional Western industry will 'wake up' to the realisation that many people derive enormous benefit from a midday nap. Sounds ridiculous? Tell that to the many millions in the Mediterranean countries who thrive on a mid-day siesta.

People in the Mediterranean and Central Americas take a siesta every working day, and this is almost certainly related to longer life expectancy and lower levels of heart disease.

In the summer of course you can go to the nearest park and try it alfresco (that's from the Italian incidentally, al fresco, meaning in the fresh air - which is another good thing for stress reduction).

Make a Cuppa

Any tea will do, but a flavoured cup of tea is even better. Experiment with different natural flavourings using herbs and spices and fruit. Fresh mint is wonderful, and excellent for the digestive system. Nettles are fantastic and contain natural relaxants. Orange zest is super (use one of those nifty little zester gadgets). Ginger root is brilliant. Many herbs, spices, fruits and edible plants make great flavoured tea, and many herbs and spices have real therapeutic properties.

Use a 'base' of green tea leaves - about half a spoonful per serving - plus the natural flavouring(s) of your choice, and freshly boiled water. Be bold - use lots of leaves - experiment until you find a blend that you really enjoy. Sugar or honey bring out the taste. Best without milk, but milk is fine if you prefer it.

Making the tea and preparing the ingredients take your mind off your problems, and then smelling and drinking the tea also relaxes you. There is something wonderful about natural plants and fruits which you can't buy in a packet. Use a tea-pot or cafetiere, or if you are happy with a bit of foliage in your drink actually brew it in a big mug or heatproof tumbler.

Fresh mint and ginger tea recipe:

Put all this into a teapot or cafetiere and add boiling water for 2-3 cups. Allow to brew for a minute or two, stir and serve. (This is enough for 2-3 mug-sized servings):

Crying

Not much is known about the physiology of crying and tears, although many find that crying - weeping proper tears - has a powerful helpful effect on stress levels. Whatever the science behind crying, a good bout of sobbing and weeping does seem to release tension and stress for many people.

Of course how and where you choose to submit to this most basic of emotional impulses is up to you. The middle of the boardroom during an important presentation to a top client is probably not a great idea, but there are more private situations and you should feel free to try it from time to time if the urge takes you.

It is a shame that attitudes towards crying and tears prevent many people from crying, and it's a sad reflection on our unforgiving society that some people who might benefit from a good cry feel that they shouldn't do it ever - even in complete privacy. Unfortunately most of us - especially boys- are told as children that crying is bad or shameful or childish, which of course is utter nonsense. Arguably only the bravest cry unashamedly - the rest of us would rather suffer than appear weak, which is daft, but nevertheless real.

Whatever, shedding a few tears can be a very good thing now and then, and if you've yet to discover its benefits then give it a try. You might be surprised.

People Most at Risk from Stress

In one U.S. study as many as 40 per cent of workers described their jobs as very stressful. While not a scientific gauge and not measuring serious stress health problems, this gives some indication as to how prevalent work-related stress is. As regards official health records, in the U.K., the nursing and teaching occupations are most affected by work-related stress, with two per cent of workers at any one time suffering from work-related stress, depression and anxiety. (The figure for teachers rises to four per cent when including physical conditions relating to stress.) Care workers, managers and professionals are the next highest affected occupations, with over one per cent suffering from serious work-related stress at any one time. UK HSE work-related stress statistics suggest that work-related stress affects men and women in equal numbers, and that people in the 45-retirement age suffer more than younger people. More socially-based U.S.A. research suggests that the following American social groups are more prone to stress (this therefore not limited to work-related stress): young adults, women, working mothers, less educated people, divorced or widowed people, the unemployed, isolated people, people without health insurance, city dwellers. Combined with the factors affecting stress susceptibility (detailed below), it's not difficult to see that virtually no-one is immune from stress. An American poll found that 89 per cent of respondents had experienced serious stress at some point in their lives. The threat from stress is perceived so strongly in Japan that the Japanese even have a word for sudden death due to overwork, 'karoushi'.

Work-related Stress Trends

Data is sparse and confused (stress statistics are also complicated by metal health reporting in the U.K.), but the statistics do indicate certain growth. In the UK HSE. statistics indicate a doubling of reported clinical cases between 1990 and 1999. Working days lost per annum appear to have been about 6.5 million in the mid-1990's, but rose to over 13 million by 2001. Greater awareness of the stress ailment in reporting no doubt accounts for some of this variance, but one thing's for sure: the number of people suffering from work-related stress isn't reducing.

Costs of Stress

UK HSE statistics suggest stress-related costs to UK employers in the region of £700m every year. The cost of stress to society is estimated at £7bn pa. (These figures were respectively £350m and £3.7bn in 1995/6 when total days lost were half present levels.)

Stress Causes

Stress is caused by various factors - not all of which are work-related of course, (which incidentally doesn't reduce the employer's obligation to protect against the causes of stress at work). Causes of stress - known as stressors - are in two categories: external stressors and internal stressors.

External stressors : physical conditions such as heat or cold, stressful psychological environments such as working conditions and abusive relationships, e.g., bullying.

Internal stressors : physical ailments such as infection or inflammation, or psychological problems such as worrying about something.

From the above, it is easy to see that work can be a source of both external and internal stressors. Stressors are also described as either short-term (acute) or long-term (chronic):

- *Short-term 'acute' stress* is the reaction to immediate threat, also known as the fight or flight response. This is when the primitive part of the brain and certain chemicals within the brain cause a reaction to potentially harmful stressors or warnings (just as if preparing the body to run away or defend itself), such as noise, over-crowding, danger, bullying or harassment, or even an imagined or recalled threatening experience. When the threat subsides the body returns to normal, which is called the 'relaxation response'. (NB The relaxation response among people varies; i.e., people recover from acute stress at different rates.)
- *Long-term 'chronic' stressors* are those pressures which are ongoing and continuous, when the urge to fight or flight has been suppressed. Examples of chronic stressors include: ongoing pressurized work, ongoing relationship problems, isolation, and persistent financial worries.

The working environment can generate both acute and chronic stressors, but is more likely to be a source of chronic stressors.

Stress Effects on Health and Performance

Stress is proven beyond doubt to make people ill, and evidence is increasing as to number of ailments and diseases caused by stress. Stress is now known to contribute to heart disease; it causes hypertension and high blood pressure, and impairs the immune system. Stress is also linked to strokes, IBS (irritable bowel syndrome), ulcers, diabetes, muscle and joint pain, miscarriage during pregnancy, allergies, alopecia and even premature tooth loss.

Various U.S. studies have demonstrated that removing stress improves specific aspects of health: stress management was shown to be capable of reducing the risk of heart attack by up to 75 per cent in people with heart disease; stress management techniques, along with methods for coping with anger, contributed to a reduction of high blood pressure, and; for chronic tension headache sufferers it was found that stress management techniques increased the effectiveness of prescribed drugs, and after six months actually equalled the effectiveness of anti-depressants. The clear implication for these ailments is that stress makes them worse.

Stress significantly reduces brain functions such as memory, concentration, and learning, all of which are central to effective performance at work. Certain tests have shown up to 50% loss of performance in cognitive tests performed by stress sufferers. Some health effects caused by stress are reversible and the body and mind reverts to normal when the stress is relieved. Other health effects caused by stress are so serious that they are irreversible, and at worse are terminal.

Stress is said by some to be a good thing, for themselves or others, that it promotes excitement and positive feelings. If these are the effects then it's not stress as defined here. It's the excitement and stimulus derived (by one who wants these feelings and can handle them) from working hard in a controlled and manageable way towards an achievable and realistic aim, which for sure can be very exciting, but it ain't stress. Stress is bad for people and organisations, it's a threat and a health risk, and it needs to be recognised and dealt with, not dismissed as something good, or welcomed as a badge of machismo - you might as well stick pins in your eyes.

Causes of Stress at Work

These are typical causes of stress at work:

- bullying or harassment, by anyone, not necessarily a person's manager
- feeling powerless and uninvolved in determining one's own responsibilities

- continuous unreasonable performance demands
- lack of effective communication and conflict resolution
- lack of job security
- long working hours
- excessive time away from home and family
- office politics and conflict among staff
- a feeling that one's reward reward is not commensurate with one's responsibility
- working hours, responsibilities and pressures disrupting life-balance (diet, exercise, sleep and rest, play, family-time, etc.)

Factors Influencing the Effects of Stress and Stress Susceptibility

A person's susceptibility to stress can be affected by any or all of these factors, which means that everyone has a different tolerance to stressors. And in respect of certain of these factors, stress susceptibility is not fixed, so each person's stress tolerance level changes over time:

- childhood experience (abuse can increase stress susceptibility)
- personality (certain personalities are more stress-prone than others)
- genetics (particularly inherited 'relaxation response', connected with serotonin levels, the brain's 'well-being chemical')
- immunity abnormality (as might cause certain diseases such as arthritis and eczema, which weaken stress resilience)
- lifestyle (principally poor diet and lack of exercise)
- duration and intensity of stressors (obviously...)

Signs of Stress

At a clinical level, stress in individuals can be be assessed scientifically by measuring the levels of two hormones produced by the adrenal glands: cortisol and DHEA (dehydroepiandrosterone), but managers do not have ready access to these methods. Managers must therefore rely on other signs. Some of these are not exclusively due to stress, nor are they certain proof of stress, but they are indicators to prompt investigation as to whether stress is present. You can use this list of ten key stress indicators as a simple initial stress test: tick the factors applicable. How did I do?

- sleep difficulties,
- loss of appetite,
- poor concentration or poor memory retention,
- performance dip,
- uncharacteristic errors or missed deadlines,
- anger or tantrums,
- violent or anti-social behaviour,
- emotional outbursts,
- alcohol or drug abuse,
- nervous habits.

Personal Stress Management and Stress Relief

If you are suffering from work-related stress and it's beginning to affect, or already affecting your health, *stop to think:* why are you taking this risk with your body and mind? Life's short enough as it is; illness is all around us; why make matters worse? *Commit to change before one day change is forced upon you.*

If you recognise signs of stress in a staff member, especially if you are that person's manager, don't ignore it - do something about it. It is your duty to do so. If you do not feel capable of dealing with the situation, do not ignore it; you must refer it to someone who can deal with it. You must also look for signs of non-work-related stressors or factors that increase susceptibility to stress, because these will make a person more vulnerable to work-related stressors. These rules apply to yourself as well. . . .

Stress relief methods are many and various. There is no single remedy that applies to every person suffering from stress, and most solutions involve a combination of remedies. Successful stress management frequently relies on reducing stress susceptibility and removing the stressors, and often factors will be both contributing to susceptibility and a direct cause. Here are some simple pointers for reducing stress susceptibility and stress itself, for yourself or to help others.

Stress Relief Pointers

- *think really seriously about and talk with others*, to identify the causes of the stress and take steps to remove, reduce them or remove yourself (the stressed person) from the situation that causes the stress.
- *Understand the type(s) of stressors affecting you* (or the stressed person), and the contributors to the stress susceptibility - knowing what you're dealing with is essential to developing the stress management approach.
- *improve diet* - group B vitamins and magnesium are important, but potentially so are all the other vitamins and minerals: a balanced healthy diet is essential. Assess the current diet and identify where improvements should be made and commit to those improvements.
- *reduce toxin intake* - obviously tobacco, alcohol especially - they might seem to provide temporary relief but they are working against the balance of the body and contributing to stress susceptibility, and therefore increasing stress itself.
- *take more exercise* - generally, and at times when feeling very stressed - exercise burns up adrenaline and produces helpful chemicals and positive feelings.
- stressed people must try to be *detached, step back, look from the outside* at the issues that cause the stress.
- don't try to control things that are uncontrollable - instead adjust response, adapt.
- *share worries - talk to someone else* - off-load, loneliness is a big ally of stress, so sharing the burden is essential.

- *increase self-awareness of personal moods and feelings* - anticipate and take steps to avoid stress build-up before it becomes more serious.
- *explore and use relaxation methods* - they do work if given a chance - yoga, meditation, self-hypnosis, massage, a breath of fresh air, anything that works and can be done in the particular situation.

Note also that managing stress does not cure medical problems. Relieving stress can alleviate and speed recovery from certain illnesses, particularly those caused by stress, (which depending on circumstances can disappear when the stress is relieved); i.e., relieving stress is not a substitute for conventional treatments of illness, disease and injury.

Importantly, if the stress is causing serious health effects the sufferer must consult a doctor. Do not imagine that things will improve by soldiering on, or hoping that the sufferer will somehow become more resilient; things can and probably will get worse.

For less serious forms of stress, simply identify the cause(s) of stress, then to commit/agree to removing the cause(s). If appropriate this may involve removing the person from the situation that is causing the stress. Counselling may be necessary to identify the cause(s), particularly if the sufferer has any tendency to deny or ignore the stress problem.

Acceptance, cognisance and commitment on the part of the stressed person are essential. No-one can begin to manage their stress if they are still feeling acutely stressed - they'll still be in 'fight or flight' mode. This is why a manager accused of causing stress though bullying or harassment must never be expected to resolve the problem. The situation must be handled by someone who will not perpetuate the stressful influence.

Removing the stressor(s) or the person from the stressful situation is only part of the solution; look also at the factors which affect stress susceptibility: where possible try to improve the factors that could be contributing to stress vulnerability. This particularly and frequently involves diet and exercise.

The two simplest ways to reduce stress susceptibility, and in many situations alleviate stress itself (although not removing the direct causes of stress itself) are available to everyone, cost nothing, and are guaranteed to produce virtually immediate improvements. They are diet and exercise.

Diet

It's widely accepted that nutritional deficiency impairs the health of the body, and it's unrealistic not to expect the brain to be affected as well by poor diet. If the brain is affected, so are our thoughts, feelings and behaviour.

We know that certain vitamins and minerals are required to ensure healthy brain and neurological functionality. We know also that certain deficiencies relate directly to specific brain and nervous system weaknesses: The Vitamin B Group is particularly relevant to the brain, depression and stress susceptibility. Vitamin B_1 deficiency is associated with depression, nervous system weakness and dementia. B2 deficiency is associated with nervous system disorders and depression. B_3 is essential for protein synthesis, including the neurotransmitter serotonin, which is necessary for maintaining a healthy nervous system. Vitamin B_6 is essential for neurotransmitter synthesis and maintaining healthy nervous system; B_6 deficiency is associated with depression and dementia. B_{12} deficiency is associated with peripheral nerve degeneration, dementia, and depression.

Vitamin C is essential to protect against stress too: it maintains a healthy immune system, which is important for reducing stress susceptibility (we are more likely to suffer from stress when we are ill, and we are more prone to illness when our immune system is weak). Vitamin C speeds healing, which contributes to reducing stress susceptibility. Vitamin C is associate with improving post-traumatic stress disorders and chronic infections.

A 2003 U.K. 18 month study into violent and anti-social behaviour at a youth offenders institution provided remarkable evidence as to the link between diet and stress: Around 230 inmate volunteers were divided into two groups. Half were given a daily vitamin/fatty acid/mineral supplement; half were given a placebo. The group given the supplement showed a 25 per cent reduction in recorded offences, and a 40 per cent reduction in serious cases including violence towards others, behaviours that are directly attributable to stress.

Vitamin D helps maintain healthy body condition, particularly bones and speed of fracture healing, which are directly linked to stress susceptibility.

Adequate intake of minerals are also essential for a healthy body and brain, and so for reducing stress susceptibility.

A proper balanced diet is clearly essential, both to avoid direct physical stress causes via brain and nervous system, and to reduce stress susceptibility resulting from poor health and condition. Toxins such as alcohol, tobacco smoke, excessive salt, steroids, other drugs and other pollutants work against the balance between minerals, vitamins mind and body. Obviously then, excessive toxins from these sources will increase stress susceptibility and stress itself.

Processed Food and Diet:

- Processed foods are not as good for you as fresh natural foods. Look at all the chemicals listed on the packaging to see what you are putting into your body.
- Generally speaking, and contrary to popular opinion, butter is better for you than margarine. This is because the fat in butter is natural and can be converted by the body more easily than the hydrogenated fat that occurs commonly in margarines.
- Fresh fruit and vegetables are good for you. Simple and true.
- Fish is good for you, especially oily fish like mackerel. Battered fish from the chip shop, cooked in hydrogenated cooking oil is not so good for you.

- Canned baked beans often have extremely high salt and sugar content. The beans are good for you, but the sauce isn't if it contains too much salt and sugar. Look at the contents on the label.
- Canned and bottled fizzy 'pop' drinks are generally very bad for you. They contain various chemicals, including aspartame, which has been linked in several studies with nervous system disorders. Many squashes and cordials also contain aspartame.
- Too much coffee is bad for you. Interestingly expresso coffee contains less caffeine than filter and instant coffee, because it passes through the coffee grounds more quickly.
- Tea is good for you. Especially green tea.
- Pills and tablets are not good for you, avoid them if you can. For example, next time you have a headache, don't take tablets, go for a run, or a walk in the fresh air to relax naturally.

Stress Management

—*Manoj Kumar Behera**
—*Dr. R.N. Mishra***

Stress is the word may people use when they are describing all the demands of their life seem to be becoming too great for them to cope with. This ability to cope with stress varies from individual to individual. But the fact is that work and stress go hand in hand. Everyone in every job experience stress. Since stress is defined as a feeling of emotional or physical tension when faced with difficult situation. Different people consider different situation as stressful. With the right attitude skills and knowledge you will be in control of your destiny, stress is the wear and tear your body experience as you adjust to your changing environment. Stress is the emotional physiological and psychological effects caused by aad internal or external mental pressure, stress is the scientific concept which has suffered from the mixed blessing of being too well known and too little understood. The real problems with stress arise when you don't do anything at all. Some people are not aware they are at risk for problems such as heart attack and stroke. Stress is so common and strikes so slowly that few people are aware of any danger till its too late. A little statistic might make this a little clearer; webmd.com estimates that 75 per cent to 95 per cent of all doctors' visits are stress related! In other words, if you have

* MBA student, PGCMS, SMIT, Ankushpur, Berhampur.
** Professor, MBA, PGCMS, SMIT, Ankushpur, Berhampur, Orissa (Biju Patnaik University of Technology).

symptoms of stress, heart disease, high cholesterol, high blood pressure, sleeping problem, headaches, faster aging, strokes, depression, ulcers, asthma, weaker immune system (reducing your natural ability to fight off infection), panic attacks, loss of memory or even obesity. . . stress can be a significant factor.

TYPES OF STRESS

Stress May be Positive

In fact some people deliberately search our stress to make life more exciting. But too much of it will prove to be harmful. When you capacities for handling stress are strong and healthy, the outcome is positive. Researches show that to a certain point, a specific amount of stress is healthy, useful, and even beneficial. This usefulness can be translated not only to performance but also to one's health and wellbeing. As stress levels increases, so does performance. However, this relationship between increased stress and increased performance does not continue indefinitely. Stress occurs when you perceive a demand on you to be greater than your resources. This can happen studying, working, dealing with events, holidays, running your own business and so on. The symptoms include an elevated blood pressure, release of hormones, and increase of tension in your muscles, rapid breathing, and sweating.

Positive Attitude Provides you the Following :

1. *The deadline that spurs (encourages) you on :* stress helps them get their work done. I've heard freelancers claim that they actually work better and have more creativity when they are stressed. Not only do they survive, but they seem to thrive when they are stressed.
2. *The target that motivates you:* Some stress can actually be good for you, as it can motivate you. But all the physical symptoms of stress can make your body weaker, breaking down its immune system. So stress for a longer period of time than a few days can be very dangerous.

3. *The challenge that inspires you:* It is curious that when most people encounter challenging periods in life they ignore the very thing that will most increase energy, improve their mood and productivity, and give them the fuel to overcome the challenge. Some of us are inspired by visualizing success. This source of self-inspiration is part visualization and part ambition, usually present among those who have a high energy-level and are willing to continually try new things and grow their careers. The inspiration is the visualization, which propels one to do more. Books like "The Secret" by Rhonda Byrne are based on this source of inspiration.
4. *An opportunity to prove:* Everyone has experienced symptoms of stress at one time or another. Speaking in public, taking a final exam, planning a wedding, and many other situations can bring on stress for just about everyone. The symptoms of stress can vary, but commonly include a pounding heart, perspiration, upset stomach, and headache, shortness of breath, fatigue and insomnia. Under normal health conditions these symptoms subside once the situation ends.
5. *Work better to a deadline:* The signal when you are in danger is a natural and good reaction that will allow you to avoid the danger. There are stresses that have a place but when does stress present a problem that affects your health and happiness. When you lose focus on what is important due to worry we may not act in your own best interest.
6. *Gives a positive emotional charge:* The first step to being able to live with the stress in your life is acknowledging that you have stress. Many people try to ignore the fact that they have a stressful life, and this is dangerous. When you ignore stress completely, it will destroy you. Not only that, but you should also acknowledge that stress has a good effect on you! You body responds to stress by giving you the energy you need to perform

when you need to. Whether it be preparing you for an important meeting at work, or giving you the energy and strength you need to finish a marathon, stress helps your body respond correctly.

Stress May be a Negative

At another level, stress may trigger a mechanism to tell you that something is wrong and start experiencing stress. When you lack the ability to handle the demands, the outcome is negative. When stress exceeds ones ability to cope, this overload contributes to diminished performance, inefficiency, and even health problems. Here is some of the negative effect of stress.

Negative attitude provides you the following :

1. *Become less efficient :* Stress is the physical and mental response of the body to demands made upon it. It is the result of our reaction to outside events, not necessarily the events themselves. Not all stress is bad. We each function best and feel best at our own optimal level of physiological arousal. We need some stress to get everyday things done. Too little can lead to boredom and "rust out" - but too much can produce "burn out".
2. *Deadlines make you panic :* Exercise is one of the quickest, easiest, and most effective ways to reduce anxiety and depression. Exercise every day for a minimum of 30 minutes. Don't ignore exercise; it is absolutely a key to recovering from anxiety. It has been medically shown that mental well-being improves in direct correlation to level of physical activity, which is great news for anxiety sufferers. Physical activity also reduces the incidence of anxiety, panic attack and phobia.
3. *Forces to eat and drink :* Pressure at work is on the increase. Business is booming for services that support stressed workers. But what can employees to do manage their own pressures at work? The first step is to put things

on paper. When people keep their anxieties in their heads, they get overwhelmed. When they make a list of all the factors that cause them pressure at work, they immediately feel that they are gaining some perspective, if not control.

PHYSICAL STRESS

The Positive Effects

1. *Success comes through :* The road to success starts within a heart that wants to be the best at something—a heart, mind, and soul that does not want to be ordinary, but extraordinary. These words of hope come from the roots of our country's heritage where ordinary people, who have a dream, work hard to achieve.
2. *Inspires others take effort :* Plain and simple, leadership is about getting others to take action. If leadership effectiveness is lacking, less than best effort is put forth. The better the leadership, the better the effort. Exceptional leadership inspires the best effort in others.
3. *Health benefits :* Research has shown health benefits of laughter ranging from strengthening the immune system to reducing food cravings to increasing one's threshold for pain. There's even an emerging therapeutic field known as humor therapy to help people heal more quickly, among other things. Humor also has several important stress relieving benefits.
4. *Provides certain values :* Change your normal routine so that you start your day being relaxed. In the morning eat a well balanced breakfast and try drinking green tea instead of coffee as it contains many antioxidants to help cleanse out toxins built up in your body. Take a brisk morning walk, followed by a hot shower to relax your tensed up muscles. After the shower do some stretching exercises before you tackle the day's problems.

The Negative Effects

1. *Bodily exhaustion :* Life span is reduced : Stress effects

on the body are myriad. Our body responds to any stressful stimulus by initiating about 1400 different activities including the dumping of a variety of chemical mediators into our blood stream. Imagine this happening on a regular basis! Stress is indeed a "Proxy Killer" as most of the time stress goes unnoticed and other secondary causes (which had been probably induced, sustained and aggravated by stress) like heart attack, blood pressure or even cancer take the blame for the person's ill-health and eventual death... Psycho-neuro-immunology has grown in leaps and bounds during the last two decades and our knowledge of the various stress effects on the body has also grown proportionally.

2. *Reduction in efficiency* : In the past three decades, behavioral interventions (chiefly relaxation, biofeedback, and stress-management) have become standard components of the armamentarium for management of migraine and tension-type headaches. Meta-analytic literature reviews of these behavioral interventions have consistently identified clinically significant reductions in recurrent headache. Across studies, behavioral interventions have yielded approximately 35-50 per cent reduction in migraine and tension-type headache activity. Although we have only recently begun to directly compare standard drug and nondrug treatments for headache, the available evidence suggests that the level of headache improvement with behavioral interventions may rival those obtained with widely used pharmacologic therapies in representative patient samples. In recent years, some attempts have been made to increase the availability and cost effectiveness of behavioral interventions through alternative delivery formats and mass communications. Recent developments within diagnosis and classification are summarized, pointing out implications for behavioral

researchers. Select future directions are discussed, which include impact of the triptans, cost and cost effectiveness, and integration of behavioral treatments into primary care settings, the place where the great majority of headache sufferers receive treatment.

3. Leads to mental stress: It may seem that there's nothing you can do about your stress level. The bills aren't going to stop coming, there will never be more hours in the day for all your errands, and your career or family responsibilities will always be demanding. But you have a lot more control than you might think. In fact, the simple realization that you're in control of your life is the foundation of stress management. Managing stress is all about taking charge, taking charge of your thoughts, your emotions, your schedule, your environment, and the way you deal with problems. The ultimate goal is a balanced life, with time for work. relationships, relaxation, and fun - plus the resilience to hold up under pressure and meet challenges head on.

MENTAL STRESS

The Positive Effects

1. Enables to understand the problem,
2. Helps to find correct solution,
3. Avoids future mistakes,
4. Creative method of finding solutions.

The Negative Effects

1. Ability gets reduced,
2. Cannot analyze correcty,
3. Wrong solutions are offered,
4. Mistakes prove costly in future,
5. Psychological stress.

The Positive Effects

1. Makes a man alert,
2. Motivates,
3. Makes sensitive,
4. Makes sensitive,
5. Makes a person human.

The Negative Effects

1. Disappointments,
2. Mental illness,
3. Frustration,
4. Loneliness.

Good and Bad Stress

A stressor is any event or situation that is perceived by individual as a threat Causing one either adapts or initiates the stress response. Therefore a stressor is a stimulus and stresses a response. To think of it another way, the stressor is the cause and stress is the affect.

Distress refers to the negative effects of stress that drain us of energy and surpass our Capacities to cope. Very often when we are taking about stress, we are referring to distress.

Sources of Stress

- Significant life adjustments.
  * Any critical life changes, both pleasant and unpleasant taking place in ones life can cause stress.
- Daily routines.
  * Daily routines such as fighting the rush hour.
  * Traffics or meeting the deadline on an important project zaps your energy. You become accustomed to your daily activities.
  * And easily overlook their cumulative effect on you.

- Unrealistic self-expectations.

  While positive self expectations motivate.

  You to realize your goals, unrealistic expectations can leads to setting yourself up For up for failure and a lowering of self-esteem.

- Interpersonal relationships.

  Both personal and professional relationships require a significant amount of effort to maintain. Poor communication.

  And inability to work with other lead to conflicts That can escalate into increased frustration And open hostility, thus leading to stress.

- No longer taking pleasure in activity that used to be enjoyable.
- Finding even simple things burdensome.
- Or difficult to accomplish.
- Feeling on edge, frustrated or annoyed, having less patience.
- A change in eating habits, either eating More or less that usual.
- Being easily annoyed by simple problems or the way other people behave.
- Marked changes in personality or mood
- Lack of energy.
- Trouble in concentrating or making decisions.
- High levels of irritabity, including.
- Abrasive, unruly or aggressive behaviour.

Stress Management

—*Sanjeev Tripathy**

Introduction

Stress can be defined as a form of tension or strain in the body or the mind for which there is no release or outlet. Stress is not something that affects us from outside. It is not something acquired only by some people are having ill fate, it is part of our psychosomatic system (Physical and mental). If it is not maintained well then it would have dire consequences. It will erode away our physical and mental strength. Stress cannot be avoided, but yes it can be avoided with proper management.

Development of the Human Psyche

The nervous system is developed to maintain co-ordination between different organs and body systems. The development of the nervous system was simultaneously being responded to by gradual development of various sensory organs

After development of the senses of perception (touch, vision, taste, smell, and hearing followed the development of memory. The body needed to retain past experiences. This was the beginning of the development of the brain. Thus, the development of the brain was a requirement of the body for the survival instinct and driven by the force of stress.

* Faculty Member, PGCMS, S.M.I.T.

The most developed living being, human being, had in the process begun thinking. The earliest human beings with such intelligence are supposed to have existed some four million years ago.

Further, development of the mind and its related faculties (emotions and psychology) was also driven by stress. It must be remembered that stress is not something connected only with the mind rather it is related to body as well as mind.

The Brain Reigns Supreme

An intelligence and consciousness about life and its environment developed, the survival instinct became the basic criterion of human perception.

At this stage, something unique happened to human beings. This was the supremacy of the brain over the body. Now, brain is the deciding factor in decision making and controlling the functioning of the body systems, all the body parts depending upon brain for their functioning.

However, since the brain is nevertheless a body organ and depends on the other organs of the body for sustenance, there is still duality in functioning. This duality may be cooperative as well as contradictory. When the body and the brain function in mutual coordination, as friends, both benefit. However, if the brain functions independent of the interests of the body, both suffer.

Because of a much better thinking apparatus, man was able to concentrate on more and more thoughts about his survival. Fears and emotions arose out of man's consciousness and apprehension of his own chances of survival in a world that was then mysterious and unknown to him. And there was death, which seemed so inexplicable and yet so certain, so inevitable. Our fears and desires, likes and dislikes, in fact all our emotions, have their roots in that primeval spirit.

It must always be remembered that among all living beings, the ancestors of man were some of the physically weakest creatures. They did not have the horns of a bull, the ferocity of the tiger or the sting of a bee. They did not have anything like claws, fangs, and tusks or superior physical strength. Without their intelligence, they were singularly unfit to survive.

Threat and Survival

We can say that we work as a response to the external stimuli. We still evaluate every signal that we receive from a threat percept. We categorize every stimulus fundamentally as either positive or negative, depending on whether it is favorable to our existence or against it. Further, emotions and feelings like love/hate, like/dislike, pity/apathy, attraction/aversion, etc are all offshoots (secondary feelings) of the primary division of the stimuli into positive or negative categories. The mind is capable of inventing its own set of expectations, interpretations and conclusions, which may not always have any relevance with reality. This is what is known as the emotional dimension of human beings.

Everyone has his own threat percept, and a different threshold of the threat percept. Different people view the same situation differently. Not everyone would take the same situation as threat in that situation. And even if there were a certainty of threat for everyone in a situation, different people would access the threat at different levels of scare. Some people get scare very easily; others take a situation as threatening only when the threat is actually serious. This could be understood as the threshold level of the survival instinct for categorization of stimuli into the negative category.

The stress factor innate in all living beings compels us to take protective action in all cases of negative categories. This is to say that when our survival is threatened or perceived to be under threat, the survival instinct activates stress in us. So we cannot stop our body from functioning in the way it triggers stress but we can certainly restrain from becoming a problem for itself.

Now, we will see how stress generated in our body and how it actually works in our body.

How Stress is Generated

Over the course of million years that process of evolution has taken place, we have been conditioned to feel safe and comfortable within certain limited physical and psychological parameters. These are safety boundaries for our body and our mind, as perceived by the survival instinct. We can also call them as our *psychosomatic paradigms.*

Whenever these limits or parameters are transgressed, whether by the body or by the mind , the paradigm is violated and the stress factor becomes active in a protective manner.

When we do not have the explanation to the situation or when we believe that the situation is negative, we feel threatened. And when we feel threatened, the stress factor comes into play, activating the mind, to devise means to help us overcome the perceived threat. Because that is what the stress factor has done for over a million years in our development, and has made us not only to survive but also evolve into what we are today.

Paradigms, or limitations, can be of the body as well as of the mind.

Paradigms of the Body

Our body is conditioned in such a way that we all have certain comfort zone, for e.g. we cannot sustain well beyond a certain limits of heat or cold. Though the temperature swings between -273° C to millions of heat but our conditioned in between 15°C to 25°C. If we would put above or below this range then we suddenly start developing stress and respond to it like wearing a sweater, switching on the fan etc, whatever tasks there in our hand.

Thus we have been given a body that is already preconditioned with certain limitations and physical attributes that can be called the paradigms of the body.

Similarly we are comfortable within certain fixed limits of all other physical factors, like humidity, light, noise levels etc. The slightest deviation from these parameters activates the stress factor. These are the limitations of our body or physical paradigms.

Paradigms of the Mind

Just as our body is preconditioned with certain attributes, so is our mind. This is so because the development of brain was a very gradual process, which took place along with, the development of body.

The fundamental attributes of the way in which intellect operates are:

- Intellect should know what is going on (Understand all the stimuli being received).
- It should be possible to categorize the stimuli into positive or negative categories.
- If a stimulus is in the negative category, there should be some solution to what is now being categorized as a threat.

The mind works continuously and keeps taking decision on the above pattern without our being conscious of it. This is the paradigm of mind.

Many of our problems are usually only in the mind. We have problems because we are not able to adjust to, or accept, things we do not like, or understand or feel apprehensive about. Strange things also threaten us. The problems are there only because things are often not as we would like them to be. It is a problem because we want the situation to be otherwise.

But once we get a proper explanation, and find that there is no threat, we are relaxed. Till we do not have the explanation, confusion and conflict remain in our mind and stress is exerted to find the answers and solutions for what our survival instinct treats as a life threatening situation.

Now let us see some of the illustrations of the paradigms of our mind:

- You hear a loud noise outside the window. You immediately want to know what has happened.
- You are walking on a street alone at night, and you see three men in the dark corner. You feel a sense of disquiet, if not fear.
- Your subordinate does not wish you 'Good Morning' one day. You are enraged.
- Your plane got delayed. You feel disgusted.
- Your son yells at you. You are annoyed.

What has happened? Why do you feel curious, angry, disturbed or annoyed when faced with such situations? Because you are not prepared for such situation when happened and also you were not accustomed to it.

These are the cases of breach of paradigm of the mind, and stress is generated to compel the mind to find solutions for such situations.

This happens because the brain creates impressions out of the external signals it receives called perception. What we see with our eyes is a sight, a picture. The message that we inferfrom this picture is our perception. Our perception is formed by not only the sight but also by memories of events associated with similar sights, and is imbued with imagination.

Now, we can have the following answers to the above illustrations:

- The loud noise was nothing but the bursting of a tier of a scooter. When you looked out of the window, not only were your fear set at rest, but you were also amused to see a person dragging the scooter.
- The people you saw were friendly neighbors. You realized this when you got somewhat closer. Your fear changed into happiness.
- Your subordinate's son had met with an accident that very morning and so he was very disturbed. Once you came to know of this fact, you were sympathetic towards him, not annoyed.

- The plane was delayed because of a bomb scare. You felt happy that you were not boarded in the plane.
- Your son has not been included in the school's cricket team. He is irritated. You came to know of this later, and encourage him to keep trying. The relationship is unaffected and amicable.

In all the above situations, it was ignorance about the full facts of the case, leading to imaginations of negative (life threatening) consequences that was the cause of the whole problem. The sensory organs of perception could collect only a fraction of the truth, or rather one aspect of the truth. What was not known was also classified in the negative category, as an apprehension, due to the creative faculty of the human mind.

Therefore, equipped with only part of the facts and supplemented with apprehensions about what was unknown, the survival instinct lost no time in concluding from the few available facts that there was a threat, and thus generated stress.

Crossing Barriers

We all have a certain physical and mental capacity for work and endurance. This is also paradigm. When we are made to do, or endure beyond our capability, the paradigm is broken, and we become tense. Stress can get triggered when we are trying to attempt something beyond our capacity, either physically or mentally.

Such situations are:

- You were made to wait for three hours to get an appointment with the doctor.
- You have to stand in a queue for two hours to get a ticket.
- There is an indefinite power cut during summers.
- Your boss wants you to complete the project report within 20 minutes.

Torments, physical or mental especially when indefinite in periodicity, can cause severe stress. Many such situations demand a capability or endurance that may be beyond you. When you have to suffer such situations, you undergo stress.

Common Causes of Stress

- Career or Business
- Finance
- Health of family members or self
- Relationships
- Prestige
- Fear of ignominy or failure
- Suppressed anger
- Frustration
- Boredom
- Despair and helplessness
- Loss of status

Symptoms of Stress

- Constant Fatigue and General lack of energy
- Insomnia and Drowsiness
- Stiff Neck and Backache
- Lack of concentration
- Forgetfulness
- Indifferent mood
- Irritability
- Desire to be left alone
- Indigestion and loss of appetite
- Weight lessor weight gain
- Frequent headaches

Silent Killer of Modern Age

The human body maintains coordination between various systems, and regulates them as well as through the endocrine system. The endocrine system can be understood as the system of hormones. Hormones are chemical secreted into the blood by endocrine glands of the body. Different kind of endocrine glands secrete different hormones for different hormones for different functions.

The two fundamental needs of any living being for survival are sustenance and protection. Sustenance is provision of food, water, air and the like.

APPROACH TO THE STRESS MANAGEMENT

Four ideal ways :

1. Body,
2. Intellect/Mind,
3. Emotions, and
4. Spirituality.

The Body

We humans began our life form as a body, and we still are primarily a physical being. Without this body we are nowhere. Taking care of this body is of prime importance to us.

The point to be noted here is that if we do not take care of the body, we can never be free of the ill effects of negative stress that always keep affecting us.

Remember - only a healthy body can continue to fight. Efforts to remain healthy not only keep you fit but also break the vicious circle of stress. For this you have to correct your lifestyle.

The three major components to stay healthy are: Diet, Exercise and Relaxation.

Diet

It has been truly said that you are what you eat. Your diet should be balanced and nutritious. All foods - including fats and oils - taken in moderations are good for health. Special attention to be given to the breakfast, which should be the most nutritious meal of the day. Lunch should be taken in moderation and dinner should be light.

The following foods need to be incorporated in your daily diet:

- Seasonal Fruits,
- Sprouts,
- All milk products,
- Garlic and ginger,
- Soya,
- Egg, and
- Water in plenty.

Apart from the above, food containing protein, fiber and carbohydrate also need to be included in the daily diet.

Exercise

These days obesity is becoming a serious problem. Many people are restoring to severe dieting to reduce weight. A little caution on the subject is necessary at this point.

If you are overweight, change the nature of your diet instead of skipping meals and starving yourself. In fact, starving to reduce weight is not good for health. It would be better to substitute oily and starchy foods with fruits, sprouts and vegetables.

Doing regular exercise, along with a change in the nature of diet, is much better option. There is no alternative to exercise. It is the best medicine.

Exercise should also be balanced and regular. The extent and pattern of exercise will depend on the age and physical condition of the person.

People suffering from any type of disease should always consult a doctor before starting any exercise regimen. The fundamental purpose of exercise should be that all parts of the body, all joints and muscles get some exercise.

If you have the facilities to play games, that is best because games not only provide you the required exercise but also a much needed break from the routine. This breaks the vicious stress cycle both at the physical level as well as at the mental level.

Walking is a very good exercise for older people but not a complete exercise for younger people.

Yoga and *Pranayama* is very good for all aspects of mental and physical stress but it need to be learnt from a guru or teacher for the initial period.

Benefits of Exercise

It keeps your body fresh, fit and healthy:

- Exercise removes toxins generated due to rush of adrenaline.
- Exercise consumes the excess adrenaline.
- It has a feel good effect, which gives positive signals to our mind and increases our feeling of well being.
- Exercise keeps the body in good shape, which increases the sense of self-esteem. People with a body in good s-hape are likely to have a higher level of self-esteem than those who have sloppy bodies. This increases the emotional or psychological strength of the person.
- A physically fit person is always in a better position to tackle his problems than one who is physically unfit.
- Exercise generates self-confidence and increases the threshold level of the survival of the instinct.
- During times of tension and stress, the exercise period affords a much-needed break from the vicious cycle of stress.
- Exercise forces body to resume all normal activities. As stated earlier, when we are under stress, the normal

function of the brain to maintain the balance between the different systems of the body gets affected. This leads to imbalance and lack of coordination between different systems. This is a major cause of several problems. However when we exercise, our body is forced to resume normal functioning, and the system gets a break from all the stress.

Train your body and mind to relax, however relaxation does not mean lying down in sofa and watching TV soap operas rather it is to give a mind a period of thoughtlessness. This is known as meditation - a state of mind when there are no thoughts and the mind is in deep rest.

Alcohol, cigarettes and drugs create an illusion of relaxation but, in reality, only suppress and thereby increase stress. Escapism does not help.

Taking care of your body will certainly require your attention, conscious effort and time. But remember, if you ignore your health today, the time will come when your body begins creating problems. Then you will be wasting much more time and money on your health, and also suffer the fear of death, which can be extremely damaging. So take care. Now!

The Intellect/Mind

Like any other body organ, the brain was not supposed to have an independent existence. But in the case of the highly developed brains of human beings, that is precisely what has happened: The brain has become the controller and master of the body. It can think on it's own, and often makes the body act as it wants. The brain exaggerates problems and dwells over them for far too long than is necessary.

When we are under tension due to any problem, the worst thing that we can do is to continuously worry about the problem. This is most harmful. On the other hand, sometimes we begin avoiding the problem. We do not want to face the problem, and so do not want to even think about it, as if by ignoring it we will be able to avoid it. We start denying the very existence of the problem. By constant auto-suggestion, we succeed in convincing ourselves that the problem does not exist.

We cannot let the mind think in any way it likes. We have to control and discipline our intellect so that we are able to think in a way that is helpful, and not damaging to us. The most fundamental purpose of pursuing the lane of intellect in stress management is to:

Shift your Focus from Problems to Solutions!

This path is to be followed by way of doing an intellectual exercise. Do this exercise by writing the various steps on paper. Why is writing it essential? Because only by thinking about it we cannot do this exercise. We are so overwhelmed by the emotions generated by our problems that we are never dispassionate about things that are likely to affect us. Hence we fail to be rational in analyzing our own problems. And the human mind is so creative that we are able to imagine problems that do not exist at all. However, when we start writing all that we think and feel, we are able to think more clearly and rationally. Writing helps in crystallizing our own thoughts. Only then can we segregate the factual from imaginary, the material from the emotional.

Step 1: Analyze the nature of your problem

- Is the problem emotional (one of mind) or is it material?
- Is the problem conceptual or physical?

Remember some of the biggest problems of our life are merely emotional in nature. Major conflicts and devastating wars that have taken place in this world have been fought for conceptual reasons, not material reasons.

Religion is a concept, a thought. Yet, today it is the cause of many of world's problems. Someone else not believing in the type of god you have been conditioned to believe in is an uncomfortable situation! Hence the religious conflicts!

If someone deprives you of your money or causes you bodily harm, then it is a material problem. Something leading you to starvation, loss of shelter or clothing is a material problem. But someone not showing respect to you, not appreciating your achievement, not accepting your point of view, not loving you. . . such situations are emotional in nature. Should we call them problems at all?

Material problems have a solution (The hungry man simply needs food), conceptual problems have no rational and amicable solutions, because you cannot reason out a solution to a problem that has its origins based not on reason but on imagination.

Conflicts created out of imagination cannot be solved by reason, unless you realize that the nature of the problem is conceptual, not material.

In emotional or conceptual conflicts, one party always wants the other party to surrender their concept in favor of the former's concept.

One is not saying that emotions do not matter. They do matter. Situations that attack our sense of pride, love, affection, justice, ego and the like do matter in life. Acknowledge these emotions, do not deny them, but always analyze them. The question is not whether it is an emotional issue or not. The question is, to what extent would you like such emotional issues to affect your life.

Do you want emotions and imaginary concepts to spoil your health, affect your working and deprive you of your happiness ?

Be your friend: *Do not let imaginary and emotional issues spoil your life...*

Step-II: Analyze the precise cause of your stress

After coming to definite conclusion about whether your tension is emotional or material, the next step is to identify the reason or cause of the tension.

The reason may be a person or a set of circumstances. And that person may even be YOU! And the set of circumstances may be of your own making! Do not be untruthful to yourself. Analyze to what extent you were the cause of the problem.

At this stage if you come to the conclusion that the problem confronting you is only conceptual in nature and that no particular person is responsible, then you should accept that no further action is required on the subject, and as such there is no reason to further waste your time or thoughts worrying about it. The exercise should end at this stage.

If you find that the problem is emotional and that someone is the cause, then it needs emotional treatment.

Step III : Write Down Consequences

If the problem is genuine and not imaginary and also you know the precise cause of the problem, you must also know what this problem is going to lead you to. Where would it end? Now list the consequences you can think of. A problem is a problem only if it has some adverse consequences.

Focus on the immediate issues, not what will happen in the future!!!

While taking care to maintain focus on the immediate issues, list the consequences in the following categories:

- Desirable
- Possible
- Probable
- Inevitable

Desirable

This is what you want. But is it possible? Delete the impossible. Don't ask for miracle.

Possible

If it is possible, then to what extent is it possible? What are the chances like? Are you worried about something that has only a one percent possibility of happening?

Probable

Are you sure it is very likely to happen? If yes, then this deserves serious consideration.

Inevitable

This deserves immediate attention.

Do not jump to hasty conclusions. Think again and review.

By doing this part of the exercise, you should zero down on the consequences that are most likely to happen in the near future.

Having listed all the possible consequences, rearrange them in order of gravity. What is the worst scenario? If the consequences are vague and remote, forget about it. If the consequences are adverse and material in nature, and within the category of probable or inevitable, that too in very near future, then go to step IV below...

Step IV: Look for Solutions

The time has come to find the solutions. What you have to do is:

- Plan for the possible and desirable;
- Prepare for the inevitable and probable.

  It is better to think about the solutions than to worry about the consequences. Your thoughts in the planning process should involve following steps:

- *Writing the options.* Planning means taking decisions on the options that are available to you. For this you must know the options. Do you have any choice of action in the given situation? What are the options? List them. What steps can be taken at various stages?
- *Listing your strong and weak points.* This self analysis has to be done one day. While the optimist exaggerates his strengths, the pessimist emphasizes his weaknesses. Be rational, unemotional, and fair in your self evaluation.

- *Seeking help from others.* Can you tackle the situation alone? Do not be shy in taking help. Do not keep problems to yourself. Mobilize other resources. Do you know who can help you? Think of all the hundreds of people you know.
- *Thinking and finalizing your action plan early.* Think! Do not be hasty. Do not take decisions on the spur of the moment. Decisions taken on impulse lack rationality, and often go wrong.
- *Starting work on the plan.* Once a rough plan is ready, do not hesitate in taking the first step. We are often so overawed by the entire problem, and so unsure of our plans, that we are afraid to even take the first step towards solution.
- *Try to solve the problem one step at a time.* You may not find the entire solution right in the beginning, because the future is always uncertain, and new situations keep unfolding all the time. Take the one best step that you can take today.

If you do not move, you may miss the opportunities that are lying in wait for you.

The Emotions

Among humans, the emotional aspect is much more complex and often overwhelming. Human emotions are the making of mind, and have tremendous element of creativity of the human intellect. Often the emotional facet predominate both the physical and intellectual aspects.

The body and the mind have direct and two-way relationships with the emotional aspect of man. The intellect and the body on the one hand help in developing the emotional build-up of man. The emotional set up, in turn, has a strong bearing on the body and the mind.

How Emotional Disturbance Create Stress

An emotional disturbance takes place due to breach of paradigm of the mind. We start expecting certain rigid responses to be followed by everyone. When this does not happen, the paradigm is broken and we wonder what has happened. Our intellect is not able to resolve the conflict between what is and what should have been.

When we are under stress, it is the emotional aspect that gets most disturbed or disoriented. The disorientation of this emotional make up, in turn, affects the brain. Not only does this disturb the normal functioning of the intellect (affects the rational thinking of the intellect), but also adversely affects us physically in the sense that it disturbs the endocrine system (The system of hormones). The brain controls and regulates the working of various systems in our body and maintains coordination and balance between our body and different systems. Mental disturbances affect this.

Even after eating food, emotional disturbance may affect the voluntary activities controlled by the brain for food processing. This may lead to disruptions in the digestive system. People under stress frequently develop loss of appetite and other digestive problems. Similarly other systems also get affected during stress.

Hence it is very necessary that you retain your emotional equilibrium. You have to make yourself emotionally strong so that you remain inured to external disturbances and do not get emotionally disturbed.

We all carry a self image of ourselves, and continuously evaluate ourselves according to that image. We feel nice and strong if that image looks good. The good image in our own eyes gives us a sense of self respect. That is what we call self esteem. Since our image depends on our own activities and achievements, the better our achievements, the higher would be our self esteem.

In today's world, we can neither solve all our problems, nor escape from them. We have to live with them, without being under stress. A higher level of self-esteem would make us more feel more secure and let us live with the problems without stress. Thus, we need to raise our self-esteem. Self-esteem does not depend only on material achievements. It all depends on how we evaluate ourselves.

We can take conscious steps to retain our sense of self-esteem, and keep ourselves emotionally strong so that problems, when they do occur, do not affect our body and mind. By taking some of the following measures, this can be achieved.

Find Diversions

- ***Keep Busy :*** An idle mind is the Devil's workshop. Being idle affords us extra time to think of the problems. In fact, we create more problems in our mind than can ever physically exist! Keep yourself physically and mentally busy. This helps to keep you away from negative creativity of the mind.
- ***Engage in social Service :*** Do something for others every day. By helping others, you actually help yourself the most in terms of increasing your own self-esteem.

Change Your Environment

If you are under stress, you may need to take more positive steps to change your environment. Here are some tips:

- Pursue a hobby
- Take a break
- Turn to nature
- Music can work wonders
- Control your anger
- Communicate
- Everyone is different
- Do not personalize issues!
- Don't be judgmental about people
- Start each day fresh
- Rationalize!
- Seek social support

The Power of Autosuggestion

Think positive. We become what we think. We can strength ourselves emotionally by seeking support from outside factors, as mentioned earlier, and also by seeking support from our own self. This is known as *therapy through autosuggestion.*

Autosuggestion means consciously giving yourself positive messages that boost your self-confidence and make you emotionally strong.

Autosuggestion does not mean self denial or self- delusion. Lying to yourself will not help. Escapism never works. Autosuggestion means telling yourself that you have done your best and will continue to do so. Through this self-interaction

Tell yourself:

- I can do this,
- I have done my part of the duty,
- This is what I have achieved.

This should be your spirit, to continue with struggle, determined that you would never surrender. Once that determination is ingrained in your psyche, that you would never accept. Defeat, the threshold level of the survival instinct would rise. You should continuously keep strengthening yourself emotionally by giving similar message to yourself.

Coin your positive slogans:

- I *will* always remain strong.
- I *will* always continue to fight.
- I *will* never accept defeat.
- I *will* never lose hope.
- I *will* never break down.
- I *will* never give up.

Spirituality

Now we will discuss how we can manage stress spiritually. Emotions followed the development of intellect and, finally, the spiritual or philosophical aspect of human beings developed. It is this philosophical aspect that distinguishes man most clearly from lesser animals.

What is Philosophy?

Action is a must to sustain life. We all act. But do we ever pause and think about what exactly is going on? About why we act the way we do? And what is the end purpose of all these activities is?

In order to understand the underlying cause of actions that are taking place around us, we need to have a philosophical perspective.

Following are the steps to be taken in the spiritual way of stress management:

- Think that everything is temporary.
- Life is a short journey on earth
- Nothing is really very important
- Everything is not in our hand
- Why to ponder over loss when you did not bring anything on earth

The Secret of Happiness

Here are some key to happiness:

- Be Humble
- Be Simple
- Be polite
- Be forgiving
- Be empathetic not sympathetic
- Be considerate
- Be caring

- Be honest
- Be generous
- Be a learner
- Be ready to admit mistakes
- Be prepared for changes - Change is the elixir of life
- Live in the present
- Don't look down upon others
- Don't gloat over other's failure
- Do not expect too much
- Smile

Do not fear anything. Seek the joy of life. Keep things simple. Generate love, compassion, harmony and forgiveness in your life. Seek the brighter side.

When you see dark clouds, look for the rainbow.... And you will always be happy.

Conclusion

The above description suggests that we need to have good health, a sound mind. At the same time we need to grow spiritually and emotionally. This will help us in getting rid of our stress and to excel in our related competency.

So *do not worry....Be happy!!!*

Refernces: 1. Times of India, 2.stress management by chunawala

Stress Management

—*Dr. K. Sriramulu**

"Every body knows what stress is and yet, nobody knows what it is".

In today's world everyone seems to be talking about stress. It has become one of the universal features of life and no one can live without experiencing some degree of stress. Right from the beginning of the civilization human organisms is subjected to stressful events like birth itself; crying, crawling, walking, talking etc. stressful experience may resulted different effects at different ages. The term stress means different things to different people. The concept appeared in medical sciences to indicate overloading of human body.

Definition

Stress is any condition that disturbs normal functioning.

—*Arnold*

Stress is defined in terms of tolerance, stressful environment which are there that are outside the normal tolerance limit of daily function at extreme level; stimulation might be perceived as pain. —*Me Garth*

It is difficult to define stress, therefore, there is no satisfactory definition of stress which encompasses the social, psychological, biological issues as they pertain to individual.

* Department of Commerce, Government Arts College, Srikakulam, (A.P.).

Types of Stress

Stress can be categorized into three kinds.

Anticipatory stress : It is one response to expected stresses. A person might give more attention to "what might happen" than to "what is happening".

Current stress : This occurs during the experience. For example, mental alertness in the midst of debate.

Residual stress : This occurs after the experience has passed.

Stress is caused by various factors their causes of stress are known as stressors. These are external stressors and internal stressors.

External stressors : physical conditions such as cold, heat, stressful psychological environments such as working conditions.

Internal stressors : physical ailments such infection or psychological problems such as worrying about something.

Causes of Stress

1. **Work overload** : Either you have got too much to do and too little time to do or job is very difficult and complex you feel which you can't handle it.
2. Poor relationships with bosses, peers or subordinates.
3. **Lack of autonomy** : Having no control and no participation in decision-making it is one of the main reasons of stress.
4. **Role conflict** : Sometimes you find yourself caught in between conflicting demands from your boss and subordinates and that can be streesful.one particularly difficult conflict can arise between your work role and role as spouse or family life.
5. **Hardiness** : Hardy people tend to involve themselves in what's going on rather than feeling alienated from it they feel and act as though they are influential rather than helpless in the face of ups and down of life and they see life as a challenge.

And there are different other causes for causing stress.

Stress Relieving Techniques

The most popular techniques are those which the people can use all the time and which act as a protection against the possibly damaging effects of a stressful life. Some of the techniques to manage stress are as follows:

1. **Relaxation** : Take out sometime each day to relax and gather strength to really feel the benefit, the impact of stress will be less on physical and psychological health. Take a deep breath, counting back from 20 to 1.
2. **Taking breaks** : Take break in work by going out, talk to someone or engage in an alternative activity.
3. **Diet and Exercise** : Take proper diet, Vitamins, minerals etc., running cycling etc 3 to 4 times a week at least 20-30 minutes, drink water, say no caffeine, listen to music.
4. **Don't let work to take over** : People develop bad habit of taking work to home with them which creates them stress whenever they see it do not take office work to home.
5. **Negotiating home responsibilities** : It is necessary to make sure that home duties are fairly distributed and time allocated for fun and relaxation.
6. **Time management** : One of the most stressful things in our working lives, that there is never enough time to get everything done, and that are can only survive working 12 hours a day.
7. **Finger magic** : One can call in a special favour and get a massage some scented oils make it more enjoyable. Massage may be on neck or forehead or legs.
8. **Discovering the yogi in oneself** : Yoga has always been remedy for stress. Daily half-hour sessions help in reducing stress.

Conclusion

Stress in more experience among the age group of 23 yrs to 35 yrs, especially working women because she has to balance her family life and work environment. Employees go through the lot of stress. Employers should provide stress free working environment and now a days most of the corporates like Satyam, Infosys, Wipro providing stress relieving techniques like *yoga,* meditation to their employees.

Management of Stress

—*Prof. N.C. Paohi**

The term stress has many connotations. Different persons have their own perceptions of what it means. Stress induces both mental and physical responses. Psychologists and physiologists have studied the phenomenon extensively since interest in the subject was generated by the researches done by Hans Seleye from 1930s.

By the late 70s and 80s a definite picture on this entity called 'Stress' had emerged. The causative factors were called Stressors. A definition of sorts had been propounded by Lazarus and Folkman that "stress is an imbalance between demands and resources and occurs when pressure exceeds one's perceived ability to cope."

With these premises a clearer picture has emerged as to the recognition and management methods of stress.

Physiologically, whenever a stressor is encountered by a person, certain metabolic responses result. Adrenaline and Cortisol are secreted in excess. The receptors to these stimulating hormones also get sensitized in the brain and muscles and other relevant organs. The heart beats faster, blood pressure rises, blood supply to muscles increases, the neurotransmitters in the brain act faster increasing the mental alacrity and the entire person gets primed up. These effects naturally affect the mental status of the person. He responds by developing fear or anger. Then he thinks of ways of resisting or overcoming the stressor, failing which he tries to

*dr.ncpadhi@gmail.com

escape from it. All these responses have been grouped under the generic term 'adaptation response'. If the stressor continues then it becomes a chronic stress. The responses will modify accordingly. One of the responses may be the way the effected person perceives this stress factor. If he thinks positively he will try to accept the challenge and deal with it rather than treat it as a threat.

There is another way of looking at the same situation. Depending upon the wisdom, experience and common sense of the person, he may analyse the stress and turn it to his advantage.

The stressors can be of varied origin. A bright light, painful stimuli, a position of loss of control over a situation like freedom, health, food, mobility, housing or authority. Even social relationships with interpersonal conflicts, deception, break ups, and defining moments at death, marriage and separation, loss of job, poverty, depression, addictions or substance abuse can all give rise to severe stress. Students and children can have problems with lack of sleep, inadequate examination preparation or achieving targets on deadlines can cause stress. Poor maternal management, sexual abuse and many other factors, too varied to be listed can create problems.

Holmes and Rahe have devised a stress scale (see below). These have been created with western populations. But they have also been suitably modified and tested on the Japanese and other nationalities and found accurate.

The importance of these findings is that stress in any form and severity can cause physical disease and mental disturbance of a serious nature. Any one under stress needs attention, both psychiatric and medical.

Non-adults

A modified scale has also been developed for non-adults. Similar to the adult scale, stress points for life events in the past year are added and compared to the rough estimate of how stress affects health.

Life Event	Life Change Units
Getting married	101
Unwed pregnancy	92
Death of parent	87
Acquiring a visible deformity	81
Divorce of parents	77
Fathering an unwed pregnancy	77
Becoming involved with drugs or alcohol	76
Jail sentence of parent for over one year	75
Marital separation of parents	69
Death of a brother or sister	68
Change in acceptance by peers	67
Pregnancy of unwed sister	64
Discovery of being an adopted child	63
Marriage of parent to stepparent	63
Death of a close friend	63
Having a visible congenital deformity	62
Serious illness requiring hospitalization	58
Failure in school	56
Not making an extra curricular activity	55
Hospitalization of a parent	55
Jail sentence of parent for over 30 days	53
Breaking up with boyfriend or girlfriend	53
Beginning to date	51
Suspension from school	50
Birth of a brother or sister	50
Increase in arguments between parents	47
Loss of job by parent	46
Outstanding personal achievement	46
Change in parent's financial status	45

Life Event	Life Change Units
Accepted at college of choice	43
Being a senior in high school	42
Hospitalization of a sibling	41
Increased absence of parent from home	38
Brother or sister leaving home	37
Addition of third adult to family	34
Becoming a full fledged member of a church	31
Decrease in arguments between parents	27
Decrease in arguments with parents	26
Mother or father beginning work	26

Adults

To measure stress according to the Holmes and Rahe Stress Scale, the number of "Life Change Units" that apply to events in the past year of an individual's life are added and the final score will give a rough estimate of how stress affects health.

Life event	Life change units
Death of a spouse	100
Divorce	73
Marital separation	65
Imprisonment	63
Death of a close family member	63
Personal injury or illness	53
Marriage	50
Dismissal from work	47
Marital reconciliation	45
Retirement	45
Change in health of family member	44
Pregnancy	40
Sexual difficulties	39
Gain a new family member	39
Business readjustment	39

Change in financial state	38
Change in frequency of arguments	35
Major mortgage	32
Foreclosure of mortgage or loan	30
Change in responsibilities at work	29
Child leaving home	29
Trouble with in-laws	29
Outstanding personal achievement	28
Spouse starts or stops work	26
Begin or end school	26
Change in living conditions	25
Revision of personal habits	24
Trouble with boss	23
Change in working hours or conditions	20
Change in residence	20
Change in schools	20
Change in recreation	19
Change in church activities	19
Change in social activities	18
Minor mortgage or loan	17
Change in sleeping habits	16
Change in number of family reunions	15
Change in eating habits	15
Vacation	13
Christmas	12
Minor violation of law	11

Score of 300+: At risk of illness.

Score of 150-299+: Risk of illness is moderate (reduced by 30% from the above risk).

Score 150-: Only have a slight risk of illness.

MANAGEMENT

The actual management of stress related problems is difficult, needs expertise of a multi-disciplinary nature. The various angles from which the approach to management may be done are listed below with a brief note on each aspect. More than one of these methods may be needed. Besides the physical illnesses like peptic ulcers, low immunity, fractures, allergy, headaches, psoriasis, heart attacks, brain strokes, diabetes complications and a host of other illnesses which can be caused or aggravated by stress, the major and most common manifestation is depression. It is laced with anxiety in many persons. And this will need urgent attention.

The obvious way to manage stress is to not allow a stressor to develop. It is easier said than done, because the victim will be stressed only if he has no control.

Methods

1. **Time Management :** For a busy person this is a very important factor. He has to prepare a time table, mark out the priority areas, give adequate tune to each task and avoid overloading. An unhurried day, well planned and schedule completed will leave one relaxed at the end of the day. Learn to say NO to requests beyond your capacity.
2. **Cognitive therapy** is done by a psychiatrist. But basically it is a method of counseling to adapt yourself to the situation, accept those over which you have no control, build self confidence and at the same time recognize the strengths of the stressor. Above all, never go into a state of 'denial'. A cool and objective, positive analysis will often solve the stress factor.
3. **Conflict resolution :** The above approach often resolves the conflict in the mind which enhances the stress. A deliberate and positive attempt should be made to resolve any conflict.
4. **Exercise :** This is a proven method of de-stressing. The quantum and timing should be sorted out so that there

is no time stress. Exercise over a period of time builds endurance, strength, immunity and self confidence.

5. **Extra Curricular Interests :** Doing something outside your field of work like social service or pursuing a hobby will distract the mind enough and instill a sense of achievement to reduce stress.
6. **Medicines :** There are now excellent drugs available to reduce depression, anxiety and mental tension. Contrary to belief they are not addictive. But these have to be taken or discontinued with consultation of the doctor. The drug treatment should be in addition to the other suggested methods. It is not a stand- alone treatment.
7. **Autogenic Training :** This method is gaining in importance with more evidence coming in of well designed studies. This includes several relaxation procedures like Meditation, Deep Breathing (Pranayam), yoga (with a proper trainer), Fractional Relaxation and natural relaxation (as at a Spa) or spending time in natural surroundings without time pressure.
8. **Music :** For those interested, music can be very therapeutic or for those artistically inclined painting or participation in art events.
9. **Alternative Medicine :** This is something which needs to be clinically proven. If it is proved to be good then it will get included hi mainstream therapeutics.

PROGNOSIS

Unless there are deep rooted psychological problems involved, the prognosis in a properly and judiciously managed person is very good. Recurrences tend to occur. Behavioral therapy may be necessary in a good number.

One of the most important factors in the management is ANGER or Hostility control. This requires special attention because it is a stressor generated by the victim himself. There are no reliable objective procedures to evaluate therapy but societal adjustment, anxiety and anger control and improvement in performance should be good indicators.

REFERENCES

Holmes TH, Rahe RH (1967). "The Social Readjustment Rating Scale". *J Psychosom Res* 11 (2): 213-8.

Lazarus, R.S., & Folkman, S. (1984). Stress, Appraisal and Coping. New York: Springer.

Selye, H. (1950). "Stress and the general adaptation syndrome". *Br. Med. J*. 4667: 1383-92.

Stress Management

—*Biswanath Patro**

—*Dr. Rabi N. Misra***

Introduction

Understanding the core factors in producing stress takes you closer to eliminating it. But since the most common conception of stress takes into account something we all know, then the definition of stress management should be obvious - except that it isn't.

We define it as our conscious knowledge of things that effect stress and the methods to divest stress harmlessly out of our body system. It is also a set of techniques that professionals do to help us in coping with various kinds of stress. Furthermore, we can also say that it is an equipping of knowledge, a conditioning, or a change of a lifestyle that allows only the most minimum instances where stress can actually set in.

Before we start, what is stress? Stress is a nervous system reaction of your body towards certain stimulus. This nervous system reaction could be easily viewed as an unconscious preparation of the body for a certain activity, like for instance releasing adrenaline chemicals onto your muscles whenever you feel alarmed, for example triggering auto response duck and adrenaline rush quickness on the muscles as you hear

* Faculty Member, P.G. Rural Management Department, SMIT, Ankushpur, Berhampur.

** Professor, P.G. Centre for Management Studies, SMIT, Ankushpur, Berhampur (Under BPUT).

and process a gunfire shot; or else shutting down some of your pain receptors while you're in a fight.

The problem with stress response is that it also triggers psychologically. Anxiety of approaching deadlines, nervousness over the outcome of a completing project, surmounting unpaid bills, or the nervous anticipation of any event, any situation that's going to happen in the near future may trigger stress response. Over time, these repeated stress experiences can severely deplete energy which could be used for other health functions like digesting meals, functioning body defense system, and such.

Returning on track, the definition of stress management is a system that is aimed to reduce stress and/or facilitate the person to cope with these instances. Because stress falls into a complex assortment of emotions and sources of them are even more profuse, the definition of stress management has become so broad, but all of them are aimed to relieve stress and divert these energies elsewhere harmless, and sometimes, even productive. All in all, the definition of stress management falls into three categories: action oriented stress management, emotionally oriented stress management, and acceptance oriented stress management.

Stress can be defined as a state of physical and mental tension caused by certain external or internal factors in a person's life.

The art of stress management is to keep yourself at a level of stimulation that is healthy and enjoyable. Life without stimulus would be incredibly dull and boring.

Life with too much stimulus becomes unpleasant and tiring, and may ultimately damage your health or well-being. Too much stress can seriously interfere with your ability to perform effectively. By analyzing the likely causes of stress, you will be able to plan your responses to likely forms of stress. These might be actions to alleviate the situation or may be stress management techniques that you will use.Stress is the most common cause of ill health in our society, probably underlying as many as 70 per cent of all visits to family doctors. It is also the one problem that every doctor shares with every patient.

Causes of Stress

The causes of stress are multiple and varied but they can be classified in two general groups: external and internal. External stressors can include relatives getting sick or dying, jobs being lost or people criticizing or becoming angiy. However, most of the stress that most of us have is self-generated (internal). We create the majority of our upsets, indicating that because we cause most of our own stress, we can do something about it. This gives us a measure of choice and control that we do not always have when outside forces act on us.

This also leads to my basic premise about stress reduction: to master stress, you must change. You have to figure out what you are doing that is contributing to your problem and change it. These changes fall into four categories: change your behavior, change your thinking, change your lifestyle choices and/or change the situations you are in. By getting to the root causes of your stress, you can not only relieve current problems and symptoms but you can also prevent recurrences. For example, if you keep becoming frustrated over arguments with your children, you might discover that the cause of your upset is not their behavior but your unrealistic expectations. By modifying your standards, you might find the children's actions no longer bother you. There are many ways to relieve stress, from going for a walk to quitting your job. What follows is a list of 10 practical and down-to-earth strategies which I have found helpful over the years for both myself and my patients. Some are simple and can be implemented quickly; others are a bit more involved. All are feasible and beneficial.

Decrease or Discontinue of Drinks

Most people do not realize that caffeine (coffee, tea, chocolate and cola) is a drug, a strong stimulant that actually generates a stress reaction in the body.

Regular Exercise

As a way of draining off stress energy, nothing beats aerobic exercise. To understand why, we need to review what stress is. People often think of stress as pressure at work, a demanding boss, a sick child or rush-hour traffic. All these may be triggers but stress is actually the body's reaction to factors such as these. Stress is the fight-or-flight response in the body, mediated by adrenaline and other stress hormones, and comprised of such physiologic changes as increased heart rate and blood pressure, faster breathing, muscle tension, dilated pupils, dry mouth and increased blood sugar. In other words, stress is the state of increased arousal necessary for an organism to defend itself at a time of danger.

The stress reaction is in us, not "out there." It provides us with the strength and energy to either fight or run away from danger and is therefore self-protective. There is only one problem: unlike a caveman being attacked by a wild animal or warring tribesman, fighting and running away are rarely appropriate responses to stressful situations in the modern world. The result is that our bodies go into a state of high energy but there is usually no place for that energy to go; therefore, our bodies can stay in a state of arousal for hours at a time.

Exercise is the most logical way to dissipate this excess energy. It is what our bodies are trying to do when we pace around or tap our legs and fingers. It is much better to channel it into a more complete form of exercise like a brisk walk, a run, a bike ride or a game of squash. During times of high stress, we could benefit from an immediate physical outlet - but this often is not possible. However, regular exercise can drain off ongoing stress and keep things under control. I recommend physical activity every day or two. At the very least, it is important to exercise three times per week for a minimum of 30 minutes each time. Aerobic activities like walking, jogging, swimming, bicycling, racquet sports, skiing, aerobics classes and dancing are suitable. Choose things you like or they will feel like a chore and you will begin to avoid them. It is also beneficial to have a variety of exercise outlets. I have never met a patient who did not feel better with some form of regular exercise - and I know I could not exist without it. For chronic or acute stress, exercise is an essential ingredient in any stress reduction program.

Relaxation

Another way to reduce stress in the body is through certain disciplines which fall under the heading of relaxation techniques. Just as we are all capable of mounting and sustaining a stress reaction, we have also inherited the ability to put our bodies into a state of deep relaxation which Dr. Herbert Benson of Harvard University has named "the relaxation response." In this state, all the physiologic events in the stress reaction are reversed: pulse slows, blood pressure falls, breathing slows and muscles relax.

Where the stress reaction is automatic, however, the relaxation response needs to be brought forth by intention. Fortunately, there are many ways of doing this. Sitting quietly by a lake or fireplace, gently petting the family cat, lying on a hammock and other restful activities can generate this state.

Meditation

Regular meditation when exercise is not possible, relaxation techniques are an excellent way to bring down the body's stress level. Whereas exercise dissipates stress energy, relaxation techniques neutralize it, producing a calming effect. As little as 20 minutes once or twice per day confers significant benefit.

Sleep

Sleep is an important way of reducing stress. Chronically stressed patients almost all suffer from fatigue (in some cases resulting from stress-induced insomnia), and people who are tired do not cope well with stressful situations. These dynamics can create a vicious cycle. When distressed patients get more sleep, they feel better and are more resilient and adaptable in dealing with day-to-day events. Sleeping-in is fine but if you sleep too long, it throws off your body rhythms during the following day. It is better to go to bed earlier. Daytime naps are an interesting phenomenon. They can be valuable if they are short and timed properly (i.e., not in the evening). The "power nap" or catnap is a short sleep (five to 20 minutes) that can be rejuvenating. A nap lasting more than 30 minutes can make you feel groggy. Patients with insomnia should be discouraged from daytime naps. Beyond these cautionary notes, sleep can be key in reducing stress.

Time-outs and Leisure

No one would expect a hockey player to play an entire game without taking breaks. Surprisingly though, many otherwise rational people think nothing of working from dawn to dusk without taking intermissions, and then wonder why they become distressed. The two major issues are pacing and work/leisure balance.

Pacing has two components: monitoring your stress and energy level, and then pacing yourself accordingly. It is about awareness and vigilance; knowing when to extend yourself and when to ease up. It is also about acting on the information your body gives you.

Realistic Expectations

- A common source of stress is unrealistic expectations. People often become upset about something, not because it is innately stressful, but because it does not concur with what they expected. Take, for example, the experience of driving in slow-moving traffic. If it happens at rush hour, you may not like it but it will not surprise or upset you. However, if it occurs on a Sunday afternoon, especially if it makes you late for something, you are more likely to be stressed by it.

- When expectations are realistic, life feels more predictable and therefore more manageable. There is an increased feeling of control because you can plan and prepare yourself (physically and psychologically). For example, if you know in advance when you have to work overtime or stay late, you will take it more in stride than when it is dropped on you at the last minute.
- There is much we can do to help patients by letting them know when their expectations (of themselves and others) are unrealistic.

Reframing

- Reframing is a technique used to change the way you look at things in order to feel better about them. We all do this inadvertently at times. For example, many people viewed the baseball strike as a personal disaster whereas others immediately realized they were going to save a lot of time and money by not hotfooting it down to the ballpark whenever the Blue Jays or Expos were in town.
- The key to reframing is to recognize that there are many ways to interpret the same situation. It is like the age-old question: Is the glass half empty or half full? The answer of course is that it is both or either, depending on your point of view. As Dr. Joel Goodman put it at The Power of Laughter and Play Conference, Toronto, 1986: "There is more than one meaning to the same reality." However, if you see the glass as half full, it will feel different than seeing it as half empty because the way we feel almost always results from the way we think. The message of reframing, then, is that there are many ways of seeing the same thing - so you might as well pick the one you like.
- One of the things we can do with patients is help them reframe stressful situations. This most often involves helping them see positives in a negative situation and

assisting them in understanding the behaviour of other people. It is best to get the patient to provide the input first (to which you can add later) by asking certain questions. The information is more meaningful when it comes from them.

- In terms of reframing the behavior of other people, ask patients why they think someone did what they did. For example, a woman's boss was acting critical and domineering towards her. "She is under a lot of pressure,' and "She is having personal problems." Performing this exercise helped the patient step outside herself and look at other possible interpretations of her boss's behavior. After that, her upset was considerably decreased.
- Notice that reframing does not change the external reality but simply helps people view things differently (and less stressfully). It should be done with a bit of preamble to explain the premise (e.g., using the glass half empty as an illustration) and only after you have acknowledged the validity of the patient's initial (stressful) interpretation. You are not trying to disrespect their point of view but only to suggest there are other, less stressful ways of looking at the same thing.

Belief Systems

- A lot of stress results from our beliefs. We have literally thousands of premises and assumptions about all kinds of things that we hold to be the truth-everything from, "You can't fight City Hall" and "The customer is always right," to "Men shouldn't show their emotions" and "Children should make their beds." We have beliefs about how things are, how people should behave and about ourselves. Most of our beliefs are held unconsciously so we are unaware of them. This gives them more power over us and allows them to run our lives.

- Beliefs cause stress in two ways. The first is the behavior that results from them. For example, if you believe that work should come before pleasure, you are likely to work harder and have less leisure time than you would otherwise. If you believe that people should meet the needs of others before they meet their own, you are likely to neglect yourself to some extent. "If you want something done right, you have to do it yourself." They do not delegate well and tend to get overloaded.
- The beliefs are expressions of people's philosophy or value system, but all lead to increased effort and decreased relaxation - a formula for stress. There is no objective truth to begin with. These are really just opinions but they lead to stressful behaviour. Helping patients uncover the unconscious assumptions behind their actions can be helpful in getting them to change.
- The second way beliefs cause stress is when they are in conflict with those of other people. A patients had a fight with his son because the child wore the same clothes several days in a row. When someone has asked where this idea originated: "Well, my mother taught me that. Everyone knows you should change your clothes every day", that this was a premise he held but one which was not shared by his son. The argument was not over the clothes themselves but merely about a difference of opinion. Once he recognized his belief was not "true," his anger diminished.
- We can do much for patients by getting them to articulate their beliefs and then to label them as such. Next, we need to help them acknowledge that their assumptions are not truth but rather opinions and, therefore, they can be challenged. Lastly, we can help patients revise their beliefs or at least admit that the beliefs held by the other person may be just as valid as their own. This is a mind-opening exercise and usually diminishes the upset the patient was experiencing.

Ventilation/Support System

- A doctor had patient who come into the office upset, talking incessantly about a problem, and feeling better when they are finished. They have told their story, cried or made some admission, and the act of doing so in the presence of a trusted and empathic listener has been therapeutic. We often do not have to say much. We just have to be there, listen attentively and show our concern and caring. On other occasions we might offer validation, encouragement or advice. But the combination of the patient being able to ventilate and our support can be profoundly beneficial.
- There is an old saying that "a problem shared is a problem halved." People who keep things to themselves carry a considerable and unnecessary burden. We can do much for patients by allowing them to ventilate or encouraging them to do so. We can also help by urging them to develop a support system (a few trusted relatives, co-workers or friends to talk to when they are upset or worried).

Humour

- Humour is a wonderful stress reducer, an antidote to upsets. Laughter relieves tension. In fact, we often laugh hardest when we have been feeling most tense.
- Humour is an individual thing - what is funny to one individual may be hurtful to another. It is wonderful when patients can poke fun at themselves. We can also do this with patients, but we have to be careful and respectful in what we say. If you think of something funny that may help the patient, say it if you feel it will ease their tension and not be offensive. Laughter is a great gift to people you care about.

Conclusion

One of the most important things we can do for patients is teach them about stress management. Even better, we can learn these lessons ourselves and then model them for our patients. Although there are many approaches to stress management, this article has taken some theoretical steps 10 ways for reducing stress that are practical, beneficial and which even busy physicians can start implementing immediately - for their patients and for themselves.

Stress Management for Students : A Study

—*Judhisthir Pradhan**
—*Arati Kumari Sabat**
—*Dr. R.N. Misra****

Introduction

The present era where we live is so swift and challenging that sometimes it seems just impossible to maintain the pace with time. Lots of works and responsibilities are to be carried out in a limited time period. When somebody deviates from the track and losses achievement, generally gets tensed. The pressure builds on him later becomes stress.

The Oxford's Advanced Learners Dictionary defines stress as "pressure or anxiety caused by the problems in somebody's life". Many scholars of different parts of the globe have defined stress in several ways. In a common sense we can say stress is nothing but any juncture of age and at any point of time a certain pressure increases which becomes stress when you fail to achieve something. People of any age group can get affected by stress. The common causes of stress are job stress, relationship problems, monetary problems, stress due to study or education etc. Stress has several adverse effects on our health. It can lead to depression and weaken the immune system and sometimes even suicide. For these reasons, people are so curious to know how to handle stress. The simplest way to cope with stress is to bring about some changes in the mindset. Various age groups adopt various tools and techniques to handle or reduce pressure.

---

* 2nd year MBA student, PGCMS, SMIT, Ankushpur, Berhampur.
** Professor MBA, PGCMS, SMIT, BPUT, Berhampur.

This chapter emphasizes on one of the most important groups i.e. the students. This paper aims to enlighten the various aspects of stress occurrence and their impacts on their life.

Scope and Objectives of the Study

Followings are the objectives of the study :

1. Students are the most important and valuable asset of the country. Hence various factors increasing stress needs close study.
2. To analyze the circumstances, situations and surroundings where a student is taking breath.
3. The problems that a student faces regularly are to be analyzed.
4. Support or guideline that a student gets from various sources is to be analyzed.
5. Action of a student during stress needs due consideration.
6. To analyze the measures/preventions that a student takes from his side.
7. To analyze the effect of the measures taken by the student.

CASE STUDY

Methods Adopted

A set of 15 questionnaires have been prepared and asked to the students of different age group over telephone or directly.

Analysis

The following outcome was noticed after the interview

Table 11.1

category	taking help from teachers	taking help from friends	taking help of parents	taking help of parents	taking help of parents
tenth	42%	19%	27%	1%	11%
plus two	9%	49%	12%	21%	9%

(Source compiled by questionnaire)

Table 2. 11.2

category	taking help of friends	taking help from friends	taking help of parents	taking help of parents	taking help of parents
graduation	21%	16%	8%	39%	16%
post graduation/mba/mca	7%	15%	3%	38%	37%

(Source compiled by questionnaire)

Physiological and Psychological/Behavioural Changes during Stress

- Speech problems.
- Impulsive Behaviour.
- Crying for no apparent reason.
- Laughing in a high pitch and nervous tone of voice.
- Grinding of teeth.
- Increasing smoking and use of drugs and alcohol.
- Trembling.
- Sweat hands.
- Dryness of throat and mouth.
- Tiring easily.
- Sleeping problems.
- Diarrhea/indigestion/vomiting/nausea
- Headaches.
- Premenstrual tension.
- Pain in the neck and or lower back.
- Susceptibility to illness.
- Loss of appetite or over eating.

Findings

- As the age grows up and the students enter into higher class/education, a gap increases between the teacher and the students. A teacher or faculty can understand the students and his problems in a better way. But due to gap and lack of proper communication, the gap increases rapidly between them.

- Mostly students in graduation level or in post graduation level take help of tobacco products, smoking and alcohol to reduce stress which is definitely a wrong way as they put their life in danger.
- In tenth class or high school level students hardly take help of tobacco related products or cigarettes (around 1%) but in +2 level it is around 18% that then and in graduation and in post graduation level it is almost double, shows that the environment where they are staying is getting worst and clearly the friend circle also getting worse.
- As per the study, around 49% students in +2 level depend upon their friends to reduce stress and this is most crucial stage where the students are getting mis-guided.
- It was observed that in graduation level around 37% (21 + 16) students are either taking help of any friend or listen to music or watching TV or remain silent. Most of the members of the members of this category are girls (around 90%) suggest that proper understanding and counseling can reduce this figure to a large extent as they hardly take the help of tobacco and alcohol.

REASONS OF STRESS

As per the study, following are the key reasons for stress among the students:

Stress due to education/academics.

- Course stress
- Examination stress
- Performance stress
- Competition stress

Stress due to relationship

- Un expected un pleasant events happen to the family
- Un expected un pleasant events happen to the family of friends circle

Stress due to financial condition

- Financial condition of family
- Deficiency in pocket money
- When borrowing or lending from friends increases

Personal stress

- Stress due to love affaires
- Misunderstanding in friends circle
- Physical problems
- Job stress

Suggestions

1. Positive attitude of family is highly essential.
2. Good friend circle is highly essential.
3. Teacher should pay key roll to solve students problems.
4. Self confidence of students can play vital role.
5. Remaining cool as much as possible will reduce stress.
6. Proper dieting helps to balance a chemical reaction within the body. Hence proper food is required.
7. Student should avoid alcohol, tobacco products and smoking for the shake of reducing stress.
8. +2 level is very crucial and needs proper care and attention especially from parents and teachers side.

Limitations

Following are some limitations of the study

1. Although the entire study revolves around the stress factors, but the student whose interview was recorded mainly belong to Orissa and samples have been taken from very few places of Orissa.

2. Due to lack of time only 80 students of various category were interviewed.
3. Most of the students are residing out of home i.e., in messes or in hostels. Hence the students who are staying with their natural guardian or family are not being talked.
4. The views collected from the students may not be 100% accurate as no evidence is there that they were in normal condition at that time.
5. During the interview some personal questions have been asked, hence there is no guarantee that they have answered honestly.
6. Percentage, fractions are eliminated.

Conclusion

Nobody can avoid stress as it is a natural biological process. But can be controlled and managed by a two way process. Some efforts can be done by students and some from the teaches, parents, guides and friends. As it is already mentioned that to control the stress one strong mind set is highly required. But as we are considering the student group of various category, hence definitely need a very good and positive mind set of the parents, teachers and guides first. One should not forget that when some body is coming for any suggestion, while listening to him/her a good frame should be maintained and the opinion seeker should not feel that his emotions and sentiments neither underestimated nor made joke.

REFERENCES

1. Patel, P. Dorab, *Stress Management and Modern Life,* Himalaya Publishing House, Mumbai, 2004.
2. Nuernberger, Phill, "A Holistic Approach" Himalaya Publishing House, Mumbai, 2005.
3. Witkin, Georgia, *The male stress Survival Guide,* New Market Publisher, 2005.

Stress Management Strategy and Techniques

—*Dr. Suresh Kumar Sahu*

Modern world is full of stress and strain. Excess stress drains out the peace from mind which leads to insomnia and this further leads to various diseases and ruins the life. It is simply because of the modern fast paced society that places incredible pressure to work hard and earn more to maintain the standard of living.

Stress plays a major role in western corporate world and regarded as costly business expense which affects both health of the employee and the corporate profit. The managers of the different organizations attempt to out bit one another to achieve the goal. Hence, the modern organizations are facing the problem of executive stress. This stress causes economic as well as human cost for the organization and society. At present stress is not uncommon in India. It has been found in Indian corporate world since 80's as Indian market became competitive.

Concept of Stress

Life is nothing but a bundle of survival instinct. This survival instinct that compelled the living beings to adjust according to their environment. The instinct to survive is the basic character of all living beings, which exerted by an internal force. This internal force is called stress.

The concept of stress is as old as human civilization. Of course, the word "stress" is derived from the Latin term 'Stringers' which means "to draw tight". Stress is not by definition synonymous with nervous tension, anxiety frustration or agitation. Thus, stress is a mental, emotional or physical reaction resulting from an individuals response to environmental pressure.

Hans Selye defines stress as "an adoptive response to the external situation that results in physical, psychological and/ or behavioural deviation for organizational participants". However different people respond stressful situation in different ways. For example, a particular situation may create different amount of stress among different people considering their capacity to coping with it. According to Bechr and Newman, "Stress is a condition arising from the interaction of people and their jobs characterized by changed within people that force them to deviate from their normal functioning".

Stress is of two types, such as (*i*) positive stress or eustress and (*ii*) Negative stress or distress.

1. **Eustress :** Eustress is the term used to describe positive stress. This refers to the healthy, positive, constructive result of stress. This stress activities and motivates people to achieve their goals and become successful in their life. In other words eustress or positive stress is highly essential for human being to survive. Hence, Hans Selye, believes that positive stress is the spice of life and absence of stress is death.
2. **Distress :** Negative side of stress is called distress. This refers the adverse affect to employees mental and physical health as well as in their work. In other words distress or negative stress is highly harmful for the individuals and for the corporates as well. Distress possess a negative force which is otherwise known as destructive stress.

Symptoms of Stress

Every individual feel stress in day-to-day life. Stress is a reaction to the external events and bring about changes in our general behaviour. The presence of stress can be estimated by analysis of certain symptoms. The various symptoms of stress can be classified into three broad categories such as:

(*i*) Psycosomatic;

(*ii*) Psychological; and

(*iii*) Behavioural. They are discussed as as below:

Psycosomatic

The word "Psychosomatic is the combination of two words such as "Psyche" which means human mind and "Somatic" which means human body. The stress occurs due to number of physical strain or diseases such as headaches, constipation, chest pain, ulcer asthama etc. which is reflected in human mind. In other words the symptoms of stress are found both in body and mind. Different persons react differently to a particular stress. The person during high level stress, loose faith in his capabilities and develops an inferior complexity which leads to low self esteem.

Psychological

Stress leads to various emotional disorders. On the one hand, its reflection is found in both body and mind of the individuals in the form of constant fatigue, lack of energy, stiff neck, backache, indigestion, loss of appetite frequent headaches insomnia, drowsiness and on the other hand it also reflects the mind in the firm of anxiety, depression, anger etc. A stressful person gets quick irritation which further leads to anger.

Behavioural

The occupational stress reflects different behavioural symptoms. The people suffering from high degree of occupational stress show cirtain symptoms such as lack of concentration, forgetfulness indifferent mood speech problem irritability, trembling, desire to be left alone, excessive drinking, smoking absenteeism etc. Work stress can also lead to less prominent symptoms such as reduced creativity, indecisive nature negativity, nervous ticks, grinding of teeth, accidents prone, increased heart beat etc. It is found that, often work stress leads the executives to high level of alcohol consumption.

Measurement of Stress

It is essential to measure the intensity of stress for coping with it by applying requisite strategy. Few instruments for stress measurement have developed by some researchers. In India mainly two techniques have been developed, which have been extensively used to measure stress they are as such :

1. Organisational Role Stress (ORS)
2. Occupational Stress Index (OSI)

Organisational Role Stress (ORS)

Organizational Role Stress technique has developed by Udai Pareek to measure stress. According to Mr. Pareek, the role (Post) assigned to an employee is linked with different parts and persons of the organization and by that assigned role the employee interacts and integrates himself with the entire organization. A lot of strain and stress is produced in the organization while the employee plays the assigned role due to clash of expectations, professional ego, self interest etc. Mr. Pareek has classified this stress into two concepts such as:

(*i*) Role Space; and

(*ii*) Role Set.

(*i*) **Role Space :** Every individual plays different roles simultaneously in this world. A particular person can play different roles in different occasions in different places on the same day, in side the organization and out side it. These roles assumed and played by the individual is called role space. But that particular person stands at the centre of the role space and other roles revolve around him. For example a person works in a company, plays the role of manager, a husband a son, a father, a neibour etc. in specific time span as and when required.

(*ii*) **Role Set :** The role played by an individual is often influenced by the expectations, professional ego, self interest and other significant roles in the organization.

Stress emerges because of inter-role distance, role stagnation, role erosion, role expectation, conflict, role overload, role isolation, personal inadequacy, self role distance, role ambiguity, and resource inadequacy. Thus Pareek developed his ORS scale measuring then types of organizational role stresses.

Occupational Stress Index

Occupation stress index technique has been developed by Srivastava and Sing to measure stress in India. This index measures stress basing upon twelve different types of occupational stresses. They are such as : (1) Role overload (2) Role ambiguity (3) Role Conflict (4) Group and political pressures (5) Responsibility for persons (6) Under participation (7) Powerlessness (8) Poor peer relations (9) Intrinsic improvement (10) Low status (11) Strenuous working conditions (12) Unprofitability.

Potential Sources of Stress

Unless and until stress is recognized properly, it is difficult to cope with it. Hence, first we will point out vulnerable stress points and this will help us to locate the potential sources of stress. The various sources of stress are classified into four broad categories. They are as discussed below.

Environmental Factors

Environmental factors also influence the stress of the employee. The environmental factors such as economic uncertainties, political uncertainties, technological uncertainties and terrorism and Maoism etc. activities have impact on the also add to the stress of the employee.

The trade cycle posses its impact on economic uncertainty. For example, when the economy is contracting people are very much anxious about their job security. Because there is every possibilities of downsizing the members of the staff which will enhance the work load, further leading to stress.

Political uncertainties, like threats and changes in Government can induce stress. The policy changes with the change in Government also enhances stress among the employees.

Technological advancement in different spheres can also cause stress. The new invention and innovations in different fields can make an employee's skills and experience obsolete. For example, the modern equipments like computers, robotics, automation and similar forms of technological innovations are a threat to many people and cause them stress.

At present terrorism is an important environmental factor which causes stress. For instance, the events like 9/11 in New York and 26/11 in Mumbai increased stresses because of the threats towards life and property. The incidence at Dantewada of Chhattisgarh, repeated events at Malkangiri, Rayagada and Koraput of Odisha made by Maoists create panic among the government and corporate employees which leads to stress.

The environment of working place is also highly responsible to cause stress such as poor lighting, poor air quality poorly designed office, lack of privacy safety hazards, excessive noise etc.

Organizational Factors

There is innumerable factors within the organization which cause stress. The organizational factors can be categorized such as

(1) Role in the organization, (2) Relationship, (3) Physical environment, (4) Job qualities, (5) Organizational structure, (6) Career development, (7) Change.

1. **Role in the organization** : Every employee plays a particular role in the organization. Role ambiguity is the confusion about the expectation of role one occupies. Role conflicts create expectation that may be hard to reconcile or satisfy. When an employee holds a middle management position or gets little management support suffers from stress.

2. **Relationship :** Stress is caused by varying expectations of significant person like superiors, subordinates, colleagues, peons and role performances dilemma as to whom to please.
3. **Physical Environment :** Working conditions like temperature excessive noise, poor lighting, poor air quality, crowding, lack of privacy, poor office arrangements etc. also cause stress in the organization.
4. **Job Qualities :** Both a quantitative job, if overloaded and on the other hand, a qualitative job if under loaded will creates stress. Various business organizations such as banks (excluding ATM service) hotels etc. now provide round the clock service because of customer needs. This type of development of business organizations will result in increasing costs to business and adds stress to employees.
5. **Organizational Structure :** Organizational structure defines, the level of differentiation in the organization, the degree of rules and regulations etc. as well as where decisions are made. Organizational policies, such as unfair performance evaluation, rotation of work, inequality in remuneration and incentives etc. create stress. Excessive rules and lack of participation in decisions making etc. might be potential sources of stress.
6. **Career Development :** Career development is highly essential for the employees and stagnation of career adds to stress. If the status of the employees of a particular class are not equal and some of them are over promoted while others do not get any promotion at all which leads to stress. Moreover, if few employees are obsolete due to introduction of modern technology also adds to stress.
7. **Change :** The change of technology, policy, management varying work, time table etc. within the organization also adds to the stress of the employee. When radical change take place one organization takes over the other organization which causes stress for the employees. The environmental change such as new colony, new town, new organization etc. also causes stress.

Group Factors

Different people belongs to various formal and informal groups. The individual members behaviour is very much guided by the group such as a department, section etc. Hence group is a potential resource of stress. The group factor can be divided into three categories. They are as such

(*i*) **Lack of cohesiveness :** Man is a social being and prefers to live in a group. This cohesiveness or togetherness provided ample satisfaction to even the employees of an organization. It is stressful, for some people, to work in a group. Hence they should learn to adjust themselves while working in a group. An employee has to maintain three crucial relationship such as superiors, subordinates and colleagues at the work place. This relationship may lead to stress for an employee.

(*ii*) **Lack of social support :** Every individual worker prefers to live in a group and at the times of stress or difficulty seeks for support from other co-workers. If an employee gets social support at the time of need then feels much better off and without such support an employee suffers from stress.

(*iii*) **Inter Group Conflict :** The conflict among colleagues or co-workers creates inter group conflict which can also lead for considerable stress for individual workers. The rising wave of physical violence and aggression in the work place also creates stress. Work place violence includes assaults, atrocity, rape, threats etc. At times manager also create stress for a particular group by proceeding inadequate direction and support.

Individual Factors

An individual employee works on an average about 45 hours a week but the problems he faces during rest (non work) hours of each week have an impact over the job. The employee's personal life is full of family problems, personal economic problems and typical personality of some people also adds to stress. Few individual stressors are presented as below.

(*i*) **Workload** : Excess work load causes stress to an employee. At present almost all organizations have downsized their work force and restructured the work. The remaining employees are required to do more work than before in a limited time. This leads to stress.

(*ii*) **Role Conflict** : The employees play different roles in organizations. Role conflict occurs where the employees face competing demands in discharging their duties. This is called role conflict. When two roles conflict with each other, it is called inter role conflict. Role conflict also occurs when an employee receives contradictory messages from different people about how to perform a work. This is called 'intra-role conflict'

(*iii*) **Role Ambiguity** : Role ambiguity occurs when employees are uncertain about several aspects of their work such as duties and responsibilities level of authority, performance expectation, area of their work etc. Mostly this ambiguity occurs when the employee enter new situations, such as joining the new organization or accepting foreign assignment because they are uncertain about task and social expectations.

(*iv*) **Life Events** : Various surveys consistently show that people lay emphasis on personal relationship and family. Personal life certainly impacts one's behaviour and performance at work place. The events like death of a spouse, marital difficulties, the breaking off a relationship, injury to one's child, failure at work, an unplanned pregnancy and similar other events can be stressful.

Economic problems is another set of personal troubles that can create stress for employees and divert their attention from their work. They are as such (*i*) economic status as measured by income (*ii*) social status assessed by educational level and (*iii*) work status as indexed by occupation.

(*v*) **Personality** : Personality includes both internal and external aspects of a person which affects behaviour. Different people experience different level of stress for the same stressors considering their personality because of three reasons such as (*i*) Self-efficiency, (*ii*) Resistance, (*iii*) Coping strategy.

The women cope with stress better than males as they can seek emotional support from others in stressful situations more easily whereas man either ignore the stressor or use less effective coping strategy.

Consequences of Stress

Stress has behavioural, cognitive and physiological consequences which is reflected on the people who experience it. The stress not only diminishes the individuals resistance but also results in adverse consequences for the organization. The continuous research by the medical scientists conclude that physiological stress could create changes in metabolism, headache, high blood pressure, high level of cholesterol, ulcer, arthritis, heart attacks etc. Stress also produce various psychological consequences such as dissatisfaction which further leads to anger, anxiety, nervousness, irritability tension etc. When multiplies it adversely affects the employees behaviour. The consequences of high level of stress are increased absence in the work place, changes in eating habits, obesity, increased smoking or consumption of alcohol, rapid speech, nervousness, insomnia etc. This further leads to low productivity, low quality, higher costs, low job satisfaction, accident proneness, poor interpersonal communications etc. in the organization. More over high level stress also impairs our ability to remember information, make effective decisions and take appropriate action.

Stress Management

The management may not be concerned when employees experience low to moderate levels of stress because such levels of stress may be functional and lead to higher employee performance. But the management is bound to take steps because the high levels of stress or even low levels continuous stress will reduce the task performance of the employee.

A mild amount of stress may benefit an employees performance but the employee may not accept it. A times even low levels of stress are untolerable by the employees. Hence, the employees and the management should be aware of an acceptable level of stress which is beneficial for both employees and management.

The O.B. researches have determined various techniques to manage or cope with stress. Of course, these strategies vary from person to person, from time to time and from place to place. The techniques of managing stress can be classified into two broad categories. They are as discussed below.

(*i*) Individual Techniques

(*ii*) Organizational Techniques

Individual Techniques

First of all, we should know the causes of stress and its effect on the individual. There are several stresses such as physical, emotional, mental, relational, spiritual and behavioural signs related to individuals. If one of the signs linked to above stressors than the employee has to adopt suitable coping strategies as soon as possible. Few self help techniques to cope with stress are discussed as below.

(*i*) **Physical Exercise** : The physical exercises such as walking, jogging, swimming, riding, cycling, aerobics, games helps the employees combat stress. These forms of exercises increase heart capacity, keeps heart bits normal diverts the mind from work pressure, releases muscle tension and also provides mental relaxation. This technique is not much expensive but requires a professional trainer to guide the employee initially.

(*ii*) **Social Support** : Man prefers to live among friends and relatives, family members and work colleagues because he gets an opportunity to drain out his stress by talk and relaxing with them. They hear to his problems and provide social support such as money, materials and emotional help at the time of need. This social support network may reduce the intensity and frequency of stress. Studies have suggested that kids and even domestic animals reduce tension to some extent.

(*iii*) **Time Management** : Many people in general, Indians in particular are poor time managers. A sincere and a better time manager can produce twice as much as the person who is a poor time manager. The basic time-management principle can help employees better cope with work stress. The time management principles are as such (*a*) Preparing daily work list, (*b*) Listing the work in preference of importance and urgency, (*c*) Arranging activities according to priorities set and (*d*) Handling most important part of job, when the employee is alert and productive . The employees should not mingle work place with home. Of course they can share problems with spouse and friends. More over instead of long vacation they should break into small vacations which will reduce stress.

(*iv*) **Positive Attitude** : An employee should develop a positive attitude to both life and work which reduce ample stress. Positive use of stress helps to regain control over the stress.

(*v*) **Rational Emotive Therapy** : This is a dynamic action oriented learning process where individuals are made to recognize the futility or irrationality of their firm beliefs and develop rational beliefs and view points.

(*vi*) **Yoga and Meditation** : The concept of *yoga* and meditation are of the Indian origin which effects the psychological well being of people who practice it regularly. According to Guru Patanjali "*Yoga* is a suspension of the function of the mind" and this act emphasis harmony of body and mind.

The *asan* is closely related to yoga which also helps to reduce the debilitating effects of stress. According to Guru Patanjali, "asan is nothing but a comfortable bodily posture". There are different types of asans varying from simple to complex form.

Meditation is a spiritual process through which peace of mind is achieved which defuses stress to a great extent.

Yoga can help employees to lead a stress free life but is required to learn asans from a trained yoga guru before they start to practice yoga. They should also learn meditation from a guru of meditation.

(*vii*) **Indian value Education:** Indian value education is also helpful to win over stress. The *Upanishada, Vedanta, Gita* etc. is very helpful for the employees to regain mental and physical vigour. Regular stress management programmes for the employees should be made particularly basing on Indian values for example the values like "karma" theory as mentioned in 'Gita' will not only reduce the work stress of the employees but also helps in developing achievement oriented motivational climate of organization.

Organizational Techniques

In addition to individual techniques the organization also develops certain techniques to reduce stress among the employees. They are listed as below

1. **Selection and Placement :** The organization is well aware of the fact that the employees with little experience are more prone to stress. The management should hire experienced individuals and place them in high stress jobs as they can perform these works more effectively. Similarly they should have new entrants and equip them with suitable training which will reduce their work stress.
2. **Sabbaticals :** Almost all employees need an occasional escape from their work place, through sabbaticals. These sabbaticals or holidays, ranging from a few weeks to few months allow the employees to relax, or to finish the personal project which is not possible in normal vacations. These sabbaticals can revive and rejuvenate the employees which reduces work stress.

3. **Wellness Programme :** These programmes focuses on the employees overall physical and mental health when the organization take care of specific health problems, health hazards or negative health habits through some work shops is called wellness programmes. For instance, they typically provide workshops to help people quit smoking, control alcohol use, lose of weight, eat better and also a regular experience programme. Of course the employees should take personal responsibility for their physical and mental health and the management is merely works as supervisor.
4. **Specific Goals :** The employees perform better when they have specific and challenging goals. The use of goals can reduce stress and uncertainties about actual job performance.
5. **Stress Audit :** Prof. D.M. Pestonjee (1999) considers stress audit as one of the effective proactive intervention to combat stress. The exercise which scientifically makes an audit of mental and physical health condition of the employees is called stress audit. This can also be done through various employee assistance programme.

Conclusion

Indian philosophy always teaches for simple living and high thinking. It always highlights about *'Tyaga'* (Sacrifice) and has paid no importance to *'Bhoga'* (Enjoyment). It also teaches that individual has brought nothing with him while entering the world and cannot take anything from world on his return, except the knowledge which he (Atma) can carry with him as atma is immortal and from there he will start his next life on his rebirth. Therefore no need for attachment for worldly commodities which will help individual to became stress free. So why and for whom he will gather wealth bearing stress. He has to perform the role assigned to him and discharge the duties sincerely without any attachment and without being hoping for the results. Thus he (mankind) can attain peace of mind and stress will never stand as a hurdle on the way of human beings to ruin health and peace.

REFERENCES

Aswathappa, K. (2007). Organizational Behaviour, Work Stress, P-290-310, Himalaya Publishing House, Girgaon, Mumbai—400004.

Gupta, C.B. (2008). Human Resource Management, Management of Stress and Burnout, P. 33.2–33.21, Sultan Chand & Sons, E-23, Darayaganj, New Delhi–110002.

Khanka S.S. (2009). Organizational Behaviour, Job Stress, P. 319-341, S. Chand & Company Ltd., Ram Nagar, New Delhi–110055.

Robbins Stephen & Sanghi Seema (2007). Organizational Behaviour, Work Stress and its Management, Dorling Kinders Ley (India) Pvt. Ltd., 482 FIE, Patparganj, New Delhi–110092.

Shukla, Ajay (2007). The 4-Lane Expressway to Stress Management, Unicorn Books, New Delhi–110002.

Index

S

S